World Food Café
Quick & Easy
Recipes from a Vegetarian Journey

World Food Café

Quick & Easy

Recipes from a Vegetarian Journey

CHRIS AND CAROLYN CALDICOTT

F

FRANCES LINCOLN LIMITED
PUBLISHERS

First published in ...
by Frances Lincoln Limited 2013

Copyright © Frances Lincoln 2013
Text copyright © Carolyn Fry 2013
Illustration copyright © Carolyn Fry and
Carolyn Fry 2013
All photography and ... preparation
by Carolyn Fry 2013
First Frances Lincoln edition 2013

A catalogue record for this book is available
from the British Library.

ISBN 978-0-7112-3296-9

Printed and bound in China

1 2 3 4 5 6 7 8 9

Page 1 Hanoi Old Quarter, Vietnam

Pages 2-3 View over Chile from
the Explora en Atacama Hotel
Paro Dzong in the Paro Valley,
Bhutan

Boy diving in Cuba; men painting
in Bangladesh; cloud berries in Lapland

River traffic on the Irrawaddy,
Burma

Contents

INTRODUCTION

This, our third World Food Café book, is a brand-new collection of quick and easy to cook vegetarian recipes we have collected on recent journeys to some of the most exciting travel destinations in the world. Most were to countries we had never been to before, where we discovered completely new tastes and styles of cuisine. Others were to countries we had not been to for many years, where we wanted to explore new areas in search of dishes we had not tried before. This is vegetarian cooking at its most delicious and imaginative. Yet even the most exotic-sounding recipes are for everyday dishes in the countries where we found them.

Regardless of how we travelled, we needed to eat on the hoof, sometimes using just what we could carry and had to cook on. Some recipes come from the home kitchens of people we met along the way; some were gleaned from ships' galleys, roadside cafés or riverside stalls; others were cooked for us in places as diverse as tents on remote mountainsides, restaurants in busy cities and pop-up kitchens at special events.

Our journey up the Irrawaddy River in upper Burma was on a converted Rhine river cruiser. In Bangladesh we navigated the Ganges Delta on an antique flat-bottomed paddle steamer. We followed the Mekong along the whole length of Laos by a combination of local boats, ferries and long drives. In Chile we combined driving with walking to cross the Andes into Argentina. On our trek to the Tiger's Nest Monastery in Bhutan walking was the only option, much of it through fresh snow. In Namibia the distances were so great that we had to use light aircraft to travel up the roadless Skeleton Coast. Driving in an open-top 1950s convertible was pure joy along the empty roads of Cuba. Our other great road trip was across Syria from the ancient city of Damascus to the even older remains of Palmyra. In Japan the fastest and most comfortable trains in the world made it possible to cover vast distances with ease, in contrast to the Reunification Express that took us so slowly along the coast of Vietnam. The slowest journey of all was following the herds of reindeer being rounded up for the winter by the semi-nomadic Sami people we spent time with in Lapland.

ALL RECIPES ARE FOR FOUR GREEDY OR SIX MODEST PORTIONS, UNLESS OTHERWISE STATED.

Bangladesh

NOT SO SLOWLY DOWN THE GANGES BY PADDLE STEAMER

Below, clockwise from top left **Fishing boats on the Ganges; cooking on board the *Mahsud*; the *Mahsud*; Natore Rajbari**

Standing on the upper deck of the PS (passenger steamer) *Mahsud*, we watched a determined sun fight its way through a cauldron of monsoon clouds and swirling river mist. Sharp rays of orange light searched out the tiny canoes of fishermen lost in the immensity of the river. On the bank silhouetted palm trees towered above villages of thatched adobe houses. Wood smoke from a hundred breakfast kitchen fires mingled with the mist. Women as brown as the bank where they knelt down to gather water bore the water away in clay pots balanced on their heads with a straight-backed grace and rhythmic swagger worthy of catwalk models.

The boat ploughed its way on through the reluctant dawn down the sluggish soupy water of the Ganges Delta. It was a scene so loaded with atmospheric drama it could have been created by special effects on a film set of a river journey into some kind of subcontinental heart of darkness.

The *Mahsud* is one of a fleet of flat-bottomed paddle steamers known as the 'Rockets' that still ply the waterways of Bangladesh daily between the capital, Dhaka, and Mongla, the gateway to the Sunderbans National Park.

Our journey had begun at sunset the night before among the epic chaos of Sadarghat, the main passenger boat terminal in the heart of Old Dhaka on the Buriganga River. Once darkness fell, we asked if we could go down below and see the on-board kitchens prepare the evening meal. In the furnace heat of the galley, deep in the bowels of the ship, some jolly cooks showed us how to make *sukto* (a yellow vegetable curry), *fulkopi* (cauliflower) with nuts and raisins and a fabulous fresh green pea dhal.

Soon after dawn we reached the fishing harbour of Barisal, busy with men delivering giant blocks of ice to the massed fishing boats. For the rest of the day we navigated the world's largest estuarine delta to a backdrop of pancake-flat paddy fields, tracts of thick lush jungle, villages on stilts, fishing nets, fishing boats, lines of hand-thrown pots drying in neat lines on the shore, farm animals and people. Always there were people, never a moment without them, busy people but never too busy to smile at strangers. In Mongla we boarded a smaller boat and set sail for the Sunderbans.

FOOD IN BANGLADESH

The popular saying 'Bangladeshis live to eat' perfectly sums up the attitude to food here, from the important daily early morning task of shopping for the freshest possible ingredients to the fine art of delicate spicing handed down through the generations. There is no doubt that Bangladeshis love their food.

At mealtimes flavours are savoured. Piling everything on to one plate at the same time is considered a crime to the tastebuds, and each dish is served as a separate course, with a definite pecking order in the way they are served. Bittersweet *shukto*, made with karela bitter gourds, usually kicks off the proceedings, as it is considered to have cleansing properties. A dhal of split or whole pulses follows, and then maybe a simple vegetable *chaat*, followed by a poppy-seed *posto*. Bangladeshis love fish but they are also very partial to vegetables. A spiced, tart, fruit *tuk* is served to cleanse the palate before the main event, pudding: milky, sweet, cardamom-spiced desserts are a speciality and it is inconceivable to end a meal without one, even if it is just a simple caramel-sweetened home-made yoghurt.

Panch phoron or Bengali five-spice – a mixture of cumin, fennel, fenugreek, mustard and black onion seeds – adds distinctive spicing unique to the region, with ground mustard seeds adding pungency. Ground spices are often blended with water before being fried in hot oil; mustard oil is the preferred cooking oil, although ghee is essential in recipes from Bangladesh's Moghul past. Ground coconut, poppy seeds, sesame seeds, dried fruit and nuts are combined to make creamy, fragrant curries, which are served alongside complex rice biryanis. If you are in hurry, there is always an inventive dhal to be had, served with crispy *luchi* (fried unleavened bread) and a garlicky mustard dip.

One thing for sure is that nothing goes to waste. The Bangladeshis have made an art out of using every bit of the humble vegetable, with recipes that transform vegetable peelings, roots and stalks into a delicious memorable meal.

In the simmering afternoon heat tiffin was served up on deck. We sipped this cooling minty yoghurt drink as we watched the day-to-day riverside life pass us by.

FRESH MINT AND YOGHURT BORHANI

¼ teaspoon cracked black pepper
½ teaspoon ground cumin
480ml/16fl oz full-fat thick yoghurt
large handful of fresh mint leaves, plus some to garnish
heaped teaspoon brown sugar
pinch of salt
2 green chillies, sliced, plus some to garnish

Toast the black pepper and cumin in a small frying pan.
    Blend with the remaining ingredients in a liquidizer with 240ml/8fl oz cold water until the mint leaves are finely chopped. Pour into tall glasses, and garnish with more mint leaves and a little thinly sliced green chilli.

Left The guardian of a shrine in Natore Rajbari

Right Fresh mint and yoghurt borhani

MOGHUL FULKOPI

5 tablespoons desiccated
  coconut
3 tablespoons sesame seeds
3 tablespoons ground almonds
I heaped teaspoon ground
  mustard
4 tablespoons ghee or butter
1 teaspoon cumin seeds
½ teaspoon turmeric
3 bay leaves

4 hot green chillies,
  slit lengthwise
1 large cauliflower,
  cut into florets
handful of golden raisins
120ml/4fl oz natural yoghurt
1 teaspoon jaggery, brown
  sugar or agave syrup
chopped coriander leaves,
  to garnish

In the half light of dusk,
the scene around the
port of Sadarghat was
like a medieval Venetian
painting. Gondolas by
the dozen delivered
passengers by the
hundred in all directions
between large country
boats laden with
cargo and powered by
patchwork sails. As the
lights of Dhaka faded,
the boat fell silent:
all the men on board
turned to Mecca and
prostrated themselves
in synchronized evening
prayer. Hundreds
of huge, battered,
exhausted-looking,
rusting hulks, heaving
with humanity in the
humid heat, jostled on
the tide for any available
inch of space on the
dockside. Among the
rabble the PS *Mahsud*,
built in 1928 in the
British-run shipyards of
Calcutta, stood out like
a proud empress from
another age.

Left Men answer the
evening call to prayer
in Sadarghat

Right River life in the
Sunderbans

The combination of ground nuts, raisins and yoghurt in this creamy cauliflower dish shows the Moghul influence on Bangladeshi cuisine.

Grind the desiccated coconut and sesame seeds using a pestle and mortar; alternatively a coffee grinder works very well. Combine with the ground almonds and mustard and toast in a small frying pan until aromatic and golden.

In a saucepan heat the ghee. When hot add the cumin seeds, turmeric, bay leaves and chillies. Stir in the cauliflower and raisins until coated with the spices. Sauté until the cauliflower starts to brown.

Add the toasted coconut mix, 240ml/8fl oz water and seasoning to taste. Cover the pan and gently simmer until the water has been absorbed and the cauliflower is soft.

Stir in the yoghurt and chopped jaggery (the sweet crystallized sap of the date palm). Gently simmer until the jaggery has dissolved. Serve garnished with chopped coriander leaves.

The watery World Heritage site of the Sunderbans is famously home to several hundred Royal Bengal tigers. The Sunderbans is an important ecosystem of mangrove swamps with a rich biodiversity, supporting populations of spotted deer, crocodiles, dolphins, giant water monitors, sea eagles, goliath herons and kingfishers. We saw all of these, except tigers of course. Tigers are hardly ever seen here, except by honey collectors, who unfortunately sometimes end up being their lunch. We eventually made our way to the open sea and had a very cautious celebratory swim in the shark-infested Bay of Bengal. What with the tigers, and sharks and snakes and swamps, it's going to be a long time before there are any tourist resorts in the Sunderbans. When we first visited Bangladesh twenty-five years ago, Biman, the national airline, was using the slogan 'Come to Bangladesh before the tourists do'; it is still using it and probably will be for some time to come.

Below Misty dawn on the Ganges in the Sunderbans

Right Bengali curry in a hurry

This green bean *shaak* is very quick and easy to prepare and as delicious cold as it is hot. It's a perfect picnic dish to make in summer when gardens and markets are bursting with beans. Serve with rice and mustard *kasundi* (see page 19).

BENGALI CURRY IN A HURRY

450g/1lb green beans, topped and tailed and cut into strips
1 teaspoon chilli powder
1 teaspoon ground coriander
1 teaspoon ground cumin
½ teaspoon turmeric
¼ teaspoon garam masala

½ teaspoon sugar
1 teaspoon salt
4 tablespoons mustard or sunflower oil
½ teaspoon mustard seeds
¼ teaspoon hing (asafoetida)
½ teaspoon cumin seeds
1 medium tomato, diced

Blanch the beans in boiling water, drain and refresh with cold water.

Mix the chilli, coriander and cumin, turmeric, garam masala, sugar and salt with a little water to make a paste.

Heat the oil in a large pan. Add the mustard, hing and cumin seeds. As soon as they 'pop', add the spice paste and stir for 30 seconds.

Add the blanched beans and cook on a low heat for 5 minutes.

Add the tomato and cook for a further 5 minutes.

GREEN PEA DHAL

3 teaspoons ground coriander	3 tablespoons ghee or butter
1½ teaspoons turmeric	700g/1½lb frozen green peas
1½ teaspoons ground cumin	4 bay leaves
1 teaspoon ground black pepper	180ml/6fl oz whole milk
scant teaspoon ground chilli	

Mix the ground coriander, turmeric, cumin, black pepper and chilli with a little water to make a paste.

Melt the ghee in a saucepan, add the spice paste and sauté for a few minutes.

Stir in the peas. When well coated with the spice paste, add 120ml/4fl oz of water and the bay leaves. Cover the pan and simmer until the peas are really soft and the water has reduced.

Remove the bay leaves and mash the peas with a potato masher until well broken down. Stir in the milk and season to taste. Simmer for a further few minutes and then serve with *paratha* or rice and green mango *tuk* (see page 20).

No meal is complete without dhal in Bangladesh. Fresh pea dhal served with hot *paratha* – an oily bread – made an unusual breakfast feast.

MUSTARD KASUNDI

Bangladeshis have an insatiable desire for mustard and this mustard and green mango dip is just as likely to be on the table as salt and pepper.

Kasundi also makes a good marinade for paneer: mix it with a little oil, coat diced paneer with it and griddle or fry until golden.

2 garlic cloves, sliced
1 dessertspoon mustard or sunflower oil
1 tablespoon black mustard seeds
1 tablespoon yellow mustard seeds
1 small green mango, peeled and chopped
4 small green chillies, sliced
teaspoon of grated jaggery, brown sugar or agave syrup
salt to taste

Fry the garlic slices in mustard oil until golden brown.

Grind the mustard seeds together to make a powder.

Place all the ingredients in a food processor and blend until smooth. *Kasundi* stores well in a sterilized jar in the fridge.

Left **Buriganga River, Dhaka**
Right **Mustard** *kasundi*

GREEN MANGO TUK

1 dessertspoon mustard or
   sunflower oil
1 scant teaspoon panch
   phoron
½ teaspoon ground turmeric
½ teaspoon ground chilli

2 small or 1 large green
   mango, sliced thinly with
   the skin on
1 dessertspoon jaggery,
   brown sugar or
   agave syrup

In a small pan heat the oil. When hot, add the panch phoron; when the spices 'pop', add the ground turmeric and chilli.

Stir in the sliced green mango, 120ml/4fl oz water, the jaggery and a pinch of salt. Cover the pan and simmer until the mango is soft, but not breaking down, and a little liquid is left.

A *tuk* is served as a palate cleanser at the end of the meal, to ensure maximum enjoyment of the sweet milky dessert to follow. It is a kind of simple chutney and we also often serve it alongside curries and *chaats*. Panch phoron or Bengali five spice is available in Asian stores, or you can mix your own using equal quantities of cumin, fennel, fenugreek, mustard and black onion seeds.

Our trip into the Sunderbans happened to begin on the first day of the annual Ramadan fast, during which devout Muslims consume nothing during the hours of daylight. The crew asked us if we would like to join them, eating only 5.00 a.m. pre-dawn breakfasts and post-sunset suppers, or to eat on our own whenever we wanted in the privacy of our cabin. We opted to join them on their fast. With a great sense of occasion we would all gather every evening with the meal spread out on the table between us and wait for the captain to declare the moment to break fast. Having eaten nothing since a very early breakfast, we were all very hungry and ate with enthusiasm. It was a great experience of really enjoying the privilege of a good meal shared. Aware how much the meal would be appreciated, the ship's cook pulled out all the stops to cook some exceptional dishes, among them a leek and broad bean *posto* and *kasundi*, a zingy mustard and green mango dip for hot poppadoms served with lashings of very Moorish fresh mint and yoghurt *borhani* drinks.

Left **Dhaka rickshaws**
Below **Buriganga River, Dhaka**

LEEK AND BROAD BEAN POSTO

Nigella seeds are also known as black onion seeds
  or *kalonji*.

6 tablespoons white
  poppy seeds
4 tablespoons mustard or
  sunflower oil
½ teaspoon nigella seeds
½ teaspoon ground chilli
½ teaspoon turmeric

2 medium waxy potatoes,
  peeled and diced
4 leeks, slit lengthwise,
  washed and sliced
110g/4oz broad beans
4 small green chillies, slit
  lengthwise

Blend the poppy seeds with a little water until a paste forms
and set to one side.

  Heat the oil in a saucepan. When hot, add the nigella seeds,
ground chilli and turmeric. When the nigella seeds 'pop', add
the potatoes and fry until golden. Add the leeks and sauté
until they start to wilt.

  Stir in the broad beans and green chillies and the poppy
seed paste. Add 360ml/12fl oz water and season to taste.
Simmer until the water has reduced and the potatoes are soft.

Ground white poppy
seed sauce, subtly
spiced with nigella
seeds, can be made
with almost any
vegetables. The cook
on our boat combined
leeks with broad beans
and diced potato.
When broad beans
are out of season, we
happily substitute
frozen beans, which
are available all
year round.

**A boy selling sundowner
snacks on the banks of
the Padma River**

Rice is simmered with milk, cardamom, raisins, jaggery and nuts to make a creamy dessert traditionally served on naming days. *Payesh* can be left to cool or served hot from the pan. Rose water also makes a delicious addition.

Natural yoghurt is eaten every day in Bangladeshi homes. A little of the day's yoghurt is added to boiled milk and left in a warm place overnight, and by morning the milk has miraculously transformed into yoghurt.

We really enjoy making yoghurt at home. It is so easy; just make sure the yoghurt you use is live. Different yoghurts make better starters than others, so if you are not happy with your first attempt try a different brand of yoghurt next time.

CREAMY PAYESH

1 litre/1¾ pints whole milk
60g/2½ oz basmati rice, rinsed
3 bay leaves
scant teaspoon ground cardamom
handful of golden raisins
jaggery, brown sugar or agave syrup to taste
handful each of flaked almonds and sliced pistachios (keep back a few to garnish the pudding)
1 dessertspoon rose water (optional)

Pour the milk into a thick-bottomed pan and heat until just off boiling. Add the rice and bay leaves and gently simmer, stirring regularly, until the rice is soft, the milk has reduced by half and the pudding has a creamy texture.

Remove the bay leaves and stir in the cardamom, raisins and jaggery to taste. Simmer for a further few minutes. Then add the almonds and pistachios (you can also add rose water at this point). Serve hot or cold, garnished with the retained nuts.

HOME-MADE YOGHURT

1 litre/1¾ pints organic whole milk
5 tablespoons live full-fat yoghurt

Pour the milk into a pan and bring to the boil, remove the pan from the heat and leave to cool until hand hot (cool enough to dip your finger in, but not too cold to prevent the process working).

Whisk in the yoghurt, cover with a cloth and leave in a warm place overnight. Hey presto! You should have yoghurt by the morning. Pour into a tub with a sealing lid and refrigerate until ready to use.

Shukto is considered a cleansing, soothing dish with which to start the midday meal. Made with karela bitter gourds, it is not to everyone's taste: sugar and milk are added to emphasize the bitter flavours. Substitute courgette or marrow for the gourds if you prefer, or savour the flavour and the opportunity to use these unusual vegetables.

SUNDABAND SHUKTO

4 tablespoons mustard or sunflower oil
2 small karela bitter gourds (or courgettes), cubed
2 medium waxy potatoes, peeled and cubed
1 small white-flesh sweet potato, peeled and cubed
3 baby aubergines, cubed
2 medium plantains or green bananas, peeled and cubed
1 teaspoon ground coriander
1 teaspoon ground mustard
2 teaspoons ground ginger
a large handful of sliced spinach leaves
2 tablespoons milk
1 dessertspoon jaggery, brown sugar or agave syrup
1 tablespoon ghee or butter
1 heaped teaspoon panch phoron (see page 20)
chopped coriander leaves, to garnish

In a saucepan heat the oil. When hot, add all the prepared vegetables (except the sliced spinach) and sauté until they start to soften.

Mix the ground coriander, mustard and ginger with a little water to make a paste and stir into the vegetables. Add 480ml/16fl oz of water, cover the pan and gently simmer until the water has reduced and the vegetables are soft.

Stir in the sliced spinach, milk, jaggery and seasoning to taste. Simmer for a few minutes longer, until the spinach has wilted.

To temper the vegetables, melt the ghee in a small frying pan and add the panch phoron. When the spices 'pop', remove the pan from the heat, stand back (it might spit a little) and then pour the spices and ghee on to the *shukto*.

Serve garnished with chopped coriander leaves and rice.

Clockwise from top left **Country boat in Rajshahi; girl carrying water in a village; man with bike on the river bank; woman collecting water in the Sunderbans**

Bhutan

SHORT WALKS IN THE LAST HIMALAYAN KINGDOM

Pages 26–27
Buddhist prayer flags

Below **Paro Dzong in the Paro Valley**

We had been riding for several hours through an enchanting forest of blue pines and wild flowers when we stopped at a lonely teahouse near a hilltop monastery. Tying the horses to a post between hundreds of multicoloured Buddhist prayer flags fluttering in the wind, our guide, Tensing, told us the path ahead was too steep for the horses, so we would continue on foot. He suggested a cup of tea and a snack of buckwheat dumplings stuffed with walnuts, mustard greens and mushroom dipped in chilli sauce before the final ascent. From the teashop terrace we could look across the valley to our goal, the Taktshang Goemba, or Tiger's Nest Monastery, spectacularly perched on a steep mountainside high above the Paro Valley. Travelling through the remote Himalayan kingdom of Bhutan sometimes felt like entering a mythical *bey-yuls*, one of the hidden valleys of Tibetan legend, where life is free from strife and discord as described as in James Hilton's classic novel *Lost Horizon*.

The trek to the Tiger's Nest was the highlight of our visit. A caravan of mules carried all our supplies, and the porters who doubled as cooks collected wild mushrooms and herbs for our evening meal along the way. The unforgettable sight of the sun rising over valleys full of fluffy clouds as white as the amphitheatre of towering peaks above them was more than enough reward for a very cold night spent camping in fresh snow.

Walking is still the most popular mode of travel in Bhutan. Towns and villages are linked by networks of well-worn trails which pass through forests and hillsides dotted with monasteries and through fertile valleys with traditional farmhouses between fields of asparagus and corn. The lower paths of our journey were often busy with local people, and once we met a group of men carrying bows and arrows walking to a neighbouring village for an archery competition.

We were invited inside antique fortified citadels, known as *dzongs,* to sit among chanting Buddhist monks in vast pillared halls lit by butter lamps, with shafts of sunlight piercing clouds of incense from a window far away. Bhutan has long been a hidden land of perfectly preserved ancient Buddhist culture, cut off from the rest of the world by the snow-covered Himalayas, subtropical jungle and a deliberate policy of isolation. This has resulted in a truly unique and mostly vegetarian cuisine.

FOOD IN BHUTAN

Rolling green hills, forests and snowy peaks in Bhutan provide the perfect ecosystem for diverse produce to flourish; an astonishing fifth of the world's plant species grow here. Climatic conditions vary from the balmy subtropical in the foothills to alpine in the mountains.

Bhutan is still predominantly rural and most villages can be reached on foot, on a vast network of winding paths. Foraged wild herbs, cherries, mushrooms, honey, ferns, nettles, taro and orchids have a vital role in Bhutanese cuisine, alongside cultivated seasonal crops such as asparagus, walnuts, apples, pak choi, mustard greens and broccoli. Invaluable harvests are dried or preserved to help people survive the snowy winter months.

Yak's milk provides essential protein and its high fat content calories to fuel the Bhutanese on long walks and in cold winters. The milk is made into butter and cheese, which characterizes many Bhutanese dishes. Cheeses range from a soft fresh ricotta-type cheese to a hard mature Cheddar type and a feta-style cheese preserved in brine. Once sealed, yak's butter can keep for up to a year. Mixed with hot tea and sugar, it makes the beloved Tibetan-style butter tea.

To say that the Bhutanese love chillies is an understatement. Large and hot, chillies adorn roofs and windows as they dry in the sun. They are regularly used as a vegetable, not a spice, and the national dish *ema dates* (chillies cooked in cheese) embodies Bhutan's favourite ingredients; add mushrooms and you have the holy trinity. Four hundred and fifty-seven varieties of mushroom grow in Bhutan and there is even a National Growers' Project.

Recipes are simply made. Onion, butter, water, chilli, simmer is the basic rule of thumb. Tibetan recipes are also popular: *momo* (dumplings), barley soup and sweet rice are common.

In high-altitude areas where the distinctive short-grain red rice cannot grow, buckwheat becomes the staple grain and is made into pancakes, noodles and dumplings.

Welcoming tiny bars, full of card and carrom players, serve snacks and locally brewed beer, whisky and fermented rice wine.

Just getting to Bhutan is an adventure. Our plane fought its way through the monsoon clouds over coastal Bengal to reveal a sparkling, snowy panorama of Himalayan peaks before descending towards Paro's tiny airport, squeezed between steep terraces of lush pasture and forested hillsides. The pilot had to negotiate his way through misty canyons by tilting the plane at extraordinary angles; we flew so close to the edge that we could see people cleaning their teeth in the morning sunshine just beyond the end of the wing.

Taktshang Goemba
(Tiger's Nest Monastery)

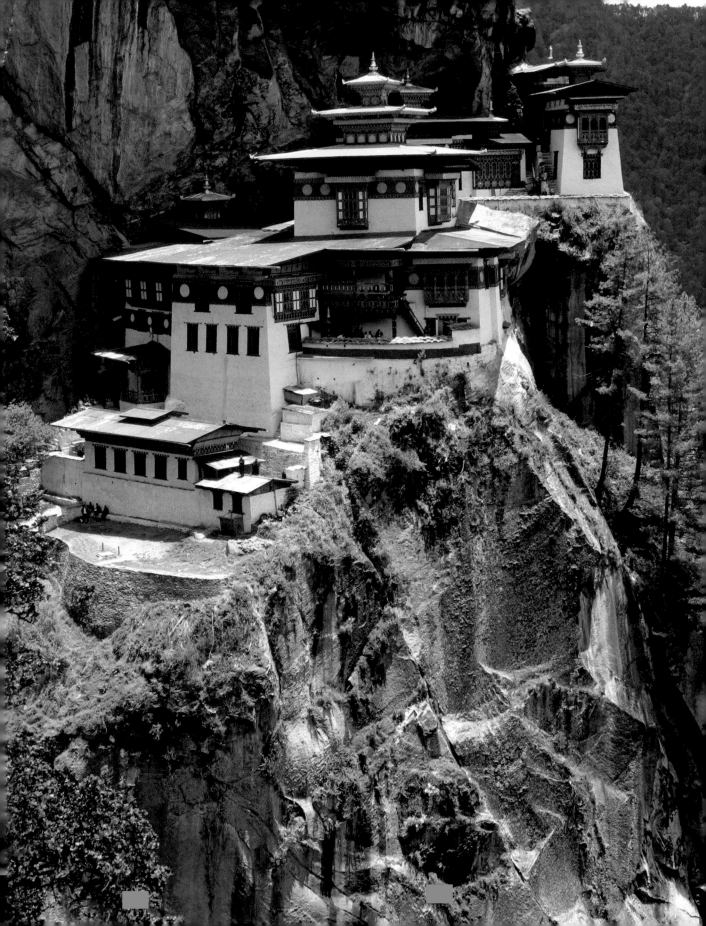

Asparagus grows wild in the subtropical valleys of Bhutan and is now grown commercially in the Paro Valley. It is cooked in a characteristically Bhutanese style: simmered in water, onion, melted butter and chilli, and topped with crumbled cheese.

This spicy garlic butter 'curry', particular to Bhutan, is incredibly simple to prepare and can be made with many combinations of vegetables. Broccoli and Buddhist meat was our favourite, but spinach and oyster mushrooms made a good second. Just follow the basic cooking instructions on the right and substitute vegetables of your choice.

Buttery Bhutanese asparagus with crumbled cheese

BUTTERY BHUTANESE ASPARAGUS WITH CRUMBLED CHEESE

4 flat tablespoons butter or ghee
2 medium red onions, finely diced
500g/1lb 2oz asparagus, snapped from
    the woody part of the stem
175g/6oz crumbled feta cheese
2 medium green chillies, sliced

Melt the butter in a large frying pan. Add the onion, asparagus and 240ml/8fl oz water; simmer until the asparagus is tender and the water reduced. Season to taste with salt and freshly ground black pepper.

Sprinkle the crumbled feta and sliced chilli over the top, and serve immediately.

BROCCOLI AND BUDDHIST MEAT TSHOEM

1 medium onion, quartered
4 garlic cloves
5cm/2in piece of ginger root, peeled and sliced
3 hot chillies (or to taste)
110g/4oz unsalted butter
500g/1lb 2oz broccoli, cut into small florets
175g/6oz Buddhist meat (seitan or marinated wheat gluten – see page 192), sliced

Blend the onion, garlic, ginger and chilli in a food processor until finely chopped.

Melt the butter and sauté the onion mixture for a couple of minutes.

Add the broccoli, Buddhist meat, 180ml/6fl oz water and seasoning to taste. Simmer until the broccoli is tender.

Almost everything about Bhutan is unfamiliar. The national dish is *ema dates*, a combination of hot chillies (used as casually as if they were green beans), mushrooms and cheese. The national flower is an extremely rare exotic blue poppy. People adorn their homes with graphic phallic cartoons, in homage to a legendary Buddhist poet and philosopher of dubious moral conduct known as the Divine Madman. The national animal is the *takin*, a bizarre herbivore with the head of a goat and the body of a dwarf bison. Men dress in *ghos*, knee-length robes fastened with a belt of woven cloth, and women in *kiras*, long dresses wrapped around a silk blouse fastened with elaborate silver hooks.

Young monks at
Punakha Dzong

This broth is a blend of Tibetan and Bhutanese cuisine. Classic Tibetan broth is enriched with the lemony herb sorrel that grows wild in Bhutan's lush landscape.

If sorrel is unavailable, you can substitute spinach leaves and a squeeze of fresh lemon juice. In the forests, wild mushrooms flourish. This recipe uses a mix of dried and fresh mushrooms.

WILD MUSHROOM, SORREL AND BARLEY BROTH

25g/1oz dried porcini (or dried mushrooms of your choice)
2 tablespoons unsalted butter
1 medium onion, diced
2 leeks, sliced
1 garlic clove, crushed
110g/4oz pearl barley (soaking the barley in boiling water for half an hour will make the cooking process quicker)

1.2 litres/2 pints vegetable stock
350g/12oz finely diced brown cap mushrooms
large handful of sorrel, sliced (or fresh spinach and a squeeze of fresh lemon juice)
2 tablespoons light soy sauce

Soak the dried mushrooms in boiling water until soft. Drain the mushrooms, retaining the liquid (making sure that any grit is left in the bowl). Rinse and slice them.

In a saucepan melt the butter, add the onion, leeks and garlic, and sauté until soft.

Add the pearl barley, sliced soaked dried mushrooms, retained mushroom water and stock. Cover the pan and simmer until the barley is soft.

Add the diced brown cap mushrooms, sorrel and soy sauce and simmer for a further 5 minutes. Finally, season to taste with salt and freshly ground black pepper.

WALNUT, MUSTARD GREENS AND MUSHROOM BUCKWHEAT DUMPLINGS

MAKES ABOUT 24

For the dough
150g/5oz plain flour
75g/3oz buckwheat flour
a good pinch of salt

For the filling
½ small onion, cubed
1 garlic clove
2cm/¾in piece of ginger root, peeled and sliced
1 hot chilli

large handful of mustard greens (or rocket)
50g/2oz walnuts
2 tablespoons poppy seeds
½ teaspoon ground Sichuan pepper
20g/¾oz sliced shitake mushrooms
25g/1oz feta cheese
40g/1½oz melted unsalted butter

To make the dough, combine the plain flour, buckwheat flour and salt in a bowl. Make a well in the middle, pour in 120ml/ 4fl oz water and mix together until a dough forms. Wrap the dough in cling film and place in the fridge while you make the filling.

Blend all the filling ingredients except the feta and butter together in a food processor until finely chopped. Mix in the feta and butter and season to taste.

Coat the dough with flour. Roll it out as thin as you dare, and then cut into 8cm/3in rounds. Place a generous teaspoon of filling in the middle of each round, wet the edges with water, fold in half and carefully press the edges together until sealed.

Cook the dumplings in briskly simmering water; they will rise to the surface when ready (after about 7 minutes). Serve dipped into chilli *ezay* (see page 40).

The path had been steadily climbing for what seemed like hours when we broke out of the forest to the welcome sight of a food stall selling buckwheat dumplings. We dipped the dumplings – stuffed with walnuts, mustard greens, mushrooms and cheese – into spicy chilli *ezay* and then, feeling replete, we set off on the final push to the monastery.

At breakfast, buckwheat pancakes drizzled with local honey, butter and lemon sauce fortified us for the day's trekking ahead. With the addition of a little finely diced red onion and chilli to the pancake batter, they are also used to accompany curries.

BUTTERMILK AND CARAWAY SEED BUCKWHEAT PANCAKES

MAKES ABOUT 12 PANCAKES

240ml/8fl oz buttermilk (or yoghurt)
150g/5oz buckwheat flour
2 medium free-range eggs, beaten
pinch of salt
butter for frying
caraway seeds

For the sauce
50g/2oz unsalted butter
juice of 2 lemons
honey to taste

Combine the buttermilk with 240ml/8fl oz water and gradually stir into the buckwheat flour. Stir in the beaten eggs and a good pinch of salt. Set to one side for 15 minutes.

Meanwhile make the sauce: melt the butter, add the lemon juice and honey, simmer for a couple of minutes and then pour into a jug.

To make the pancakes, melt a little butter in a non-stick pan and ladle in enough batter to coat the bottom of the pan. Sprinkle with caraway seeds. When the batter has set, flip and cook the other side. Repeat the process until all the batter is used up.

Serve drizzled with the lemon and honey sauce.

Left A teaching monk at Punakha Dzong Monastery
Right Covered bridge over the river in Paro

PAK CHOI, LEEK AND OMELETTE BUCKWHEAT NOODLE STIR-FRY

250g/9oz buckwheat or
    udon noodles
3 medium free-range eggs
1 tablespoon unsalted butter,
    plus a knob for frying
1½ tablespoons sesame oil
1 small onion, finely diced
3 garlic cloves, crushed
3cm/1¼ in piece of ginger
    root, peeled and grated
3 hot chillies, sliced
2 leeks, sliced
2 large heads pak choi, sliced
    (or 225g/8oz sliced kale
    or spinach)

225g/8oz sliced fresh
    shitake mushrooms
1 large ripe tomato, diced
2 tablespoons Shaoxing wine
    or dry sherry
120ml/4fl oz vegetable stock
1 tablespoon light soy sauce
6 spring onions, sliced

To garnish
handful of grated mooli
    (white radish)
chopped coriander leaves

Cook the buckwheat noodles in salted water until soft. Drain, rinse well and set to one side.

Make an omelette: beat the eggs with a little salt and pepper, pour into a hot frying pan with a knob of melted butter and fry until golden on both sides. Turn the finished omelette on to a board and cut into strips.

Heat the sesame oil and remaining butter in a wok; add the onion, garlic, ginger, chilli and leeks, and sauté until soft.

Add the sliced pak choi, shitake mushrooms, tomato, Shaoxing wine, vegetable stock and soy sauce. Simmer until the pak choi is tender.

Stir in the cooked buckwheat noodles and spring onions. Serve topped with the omelette strips, mooli and coriander leaves.

In high-altitude areas buckwheat replaces red rice as the staple grain. Hand-ground buckwheat flour is made into thin noodles, similar to the *soba* noodles that accompany stir-fries and curries.

Locally brewed rice wine is added to flavour stir-fries. Chinese Shaoxing rice wine is similar and dry sherry also makes a good substitute.

Pak choi, leek and omelette buckwheat noodle stir-fry

CHILLI DATSHI

350g/12oz large green chillies
1 medium onion, diced
4 garlic cloves, crushed
4 teaspoons unsalted butter

350g/12oz feta cheese
handful of chopped
  coriander leaves,
  to garnish

Cut the chillies in half and scrape out the seeds. Slice in eighths lengthwise (if you are using peppers as well, cut these to a similar size).

Place the chillies in a pan with the diced onion, garlic, butter and 240ml/8fl oz water. (Now is a good time to wash your hands if you want to avoid any nasty accidents.) Cook at a brisk simmer until the chillies are soft, and season to taste.

Reduce the heat and crumble the feta cheese into the pan. Carefully stir until the cheese has melted, taking care not to boil the cheese. Garnish with chopped coriander. Serve with lightly cooked green vegetables and red rice (short-grain brown rice makes a good substitute for red rice).

CHILLI EZAY

handful of dried jalapeño
  chilli peppers (or medium-
  sized and spiced dried red
  chillies)
1 small red onion, diced

3cm/1¼in piece of ginger
  root, peeled and sliced
1 tablespoon ground Sichuan
  pepper
1 largish ripe tomato, diced
salt to taste

Soak the dried chillies in boiling water until soft.

Drain the chillies and blend in a food processor with the remaining ingredients until a thickish salsa forms.

Hold on to your hats! Chilli *datshi* is a heady mix of hot chillies and melted cheese. Beware the chillies: they are used as a vegetable, not a seasoning – a unique combination of flavours, but not for the faint-hearted. However, even if you are not a chilli lover there are still ways to enjoy this recipe: spicy, large green chillies, similar to jalapeños, are traditionally used but you can substitute a milder chilli (with the seeds removed) or dilute the burn by mixing half the quantity of chillies with Romano peppers.

This recipe uses a crumbly, salty yak's milk cheese, but feta cheese makes a good alternative. Chilli *datshi* is quite rich, so quantities aren't huge.

Buddhist prayer flags above the Paro Valley

Despite chillies being in every dish, the Bhutanese think nothing of serving a large portion of fiery chilli *ezay* with every meal. Smear it on to buckwheat dumplings or dollop on to any *tshoem* (see page 33). Remember that you can always customize the *ezay* to your taste by using less spicy chillies. Of course some like it hot, and spicier chillies might be your preference.

The Bhutanese are not fond of change. When the first ever traffic light was introduced at Thimpu's only major road intersection, there were public demonstrations that resulted in its being replaced by a policeman with white gloves, who performs a sort of ballet version of traffic control.

The current monastic dynasty began in 1907, when regional chieftains and high lamas elected Ugyen Wangchuck as the supreme hereditary ruler of Bhutan. Four Wangchucks and a hundred years on, things are about to change. In 2005, Jigme Singye Wangchuck, famous for being more concerned about his people's Gross National Happiness than his kingdom's GDP, announced his imminent abdication and the introduction of a constitutional democracy. Since then his son has taken the throne as a constitutional monarch and change is accelerating with the introduction of television, more roads and cars, and contact with the outside world.

MUSHROOM AND POTATO DATSHI

5 medium-sized waxy
  potatoes, peeled, cut in
  half lengthwise and then
  into ½cm/¼in semicircles
1 medium red onion, diced
1 tablespoon unsalted butter
1½ teaspoons chilli flakes (or
  to taste)

200g/7oz thickly sliced
  shitake or oyster
  mushrooms
110g/4oz grated mature
  Cheddar
25g/1oz grated Parmesan
  cheese
4 spring onions, thinly sliced

Place the potato, onion, butter and 360ml/12fl oz water in a
pan, cover and gently simmer until the potato is just cooked.

Add the chilli flakes and sliced mushrooms, and simmer for a
further couple of minutes.

Sprinkle the grated Cheddar and Parmesan over the top
and carefully stir together until the cheese has melted. Finally
season to taste and top with sliced spring onions.

More cheese, but after
a long day filled with
hiking and archery, it's
just what the doctor
ordered. The Bhutanese
have thought of every
possible cheese and
chilli combination,
but amazingly they all
taste quite different.

Mushroom and
potato *datshi* is made
with a mature, hard
yak's milk cheese;
the best substitute
we have found is a
mix of strong, mature
Cheddar and Parmesan
cheese. You can use
any type of mushroom
in this dish, but oyster
or shitake are the most
authentic option.

At our mid-afternoon tea stop, our cook prepared diced local apples and basmati rice fried in spiced honey butter, with butter tea to drink.

Left **The confluence of two rivers in the Punakha Valley**

Below **A monk running late for prayers**

APPLE, SAFFRON AND HONEY BUTTER RICE

60g/2½oz unsalted butter
pinch of salt
1 teaspoon ground cardamom
3 large pinches of saffron
2 rosy dessert apples, diced
60g/2½oz golden raisins

2 good tablespoons runny honey
725ml/1¼ pints cooked basmati rice (measured in a measuring jug)
plain natural yoghurt, to serve

Melt the butter in a saucepan. Stir in the salt, cardamom and saffron.

Add the diced apple, raisins and honey. Gently simmer until the apples are soft.

Add the rice and cook, stirring constantly, until piping hot. Serve topped with a dollop of natural yoghurt.

Burma

A MONSOON BOAT RIDE
UP THE IRRAWADDY

Burma featured regularly in our travel itineraries of the 1970s and 1980s. Despite the challenge of having to rush about on a seven-day visa, we were lured back there every year by the vast, timeless, dramatic landscapes, the thousands of evocative ancient ruins, the living Buddhist culture and the delicious cuisine. However, it was always the gentle, generous spirt of the Burmese people that made the most lasting impression. When we returned recently, after more than twenty-five years away, it was wonderful to find among the Burmese a new sense of optimism for a better future. Little else had changed: it is still a unique land, almost completely unconnected to the rest of the world, as though it exists in a parallel universe.

Visas are more generous now, so we were able to travel far beyond the usual Rangoon/Mandalay/Bagan/Inle Lake circuit (although we revisited all of them) and get right up into upper Burma. This time we timed our visit to be there during the monsoon, when the Irrawaddy River is in spate and it is possible to travel by boat via Katha, where Eric Blair (George Orwell) was stationed as a colonial policeman, all the way to Bharmo near the Chinese border. The further we went up river, the better it got. Every morning we were treated to spectacular sunrises as the sun burnt its way through swirling river mists until the air was crystal clear.

Travelling by boat proved an excellent way of collecting new recipes, as we had the advantage of being able both to spend time with the on-board chefs and to try regional delicaces in all the places we stopped at on the journey. We began every day with a traditional Burmese breakfast of *mohinga* (pronounced moun-hinga), an aromatic noodle soup served with a variety of side dishes like hard-boiled eggs, limes, fried garlic, spring onions, chickpeas, chillies and mung bean patties. In villages on the river bank we snacked on piping hot split pea fritters straight from sizzling woks. Every evening we anchored in mid-river as the setting sun seemed to set the moody monsoon clouds on fire, and then dined on hearty soups, zesty salads and succulent curries with sesame rice.

Pages 44–45 **A misty sunrise over the pagodas of Bagan**
Left **Dawn on the Irrawaddy**

FOOD IN BURMA

Burma is populated by a variety of different ethnic and cultural groups – in particular the Shans, the Mons, the Chins, the Karens and the Burmans. Each group has its own culinary style; however, there are some dishes that have become ubiquitous throughout the country. Most Burmese cooking is influenced by its two largest neighbours, India and China.

Fertile soil and good water resources ensure that in the markets of Burma fruit and vegetables are abundant all year round. Rice is the staple ingredient of most meals and served simply steamed, cooked with spices, coconut and sesame, or transformed into rice noodles. Ginger, garlic and onion pounded together with turmeric and chilli form the base of most soups and curries. Indian and Chinese influences are combined with home-grown flavours to create a uniquely Burmese cuisine. Sweet, spiced milky black Indian-style chai and Chinese green tea are equally popular.

A typical meal consists of soup, salad, curry and vegetables with an array of toppings such as crisp fried onions and garlic. All dishes are served together, laid out on a low round table just big enough so that no one has to stretch; and, with much chatter, family and friends gather round, seated on mats, to share the delicious food on offer.

Soup is indispensable, served in a single central bowl for all to share alongside the main meal. Fresh fruit and raw vegetables are dressed with lime and chilli to create spicy, refreshing salads. Curries tend to be aromatic but mild, and as a sign of respect elderly family members and guests are always offered the first serving. Knives are never used at the table and the general rule is if you want more rice, always leave a little in the serving bowl; if the bowl is left empty, it is taken for granted that you are finished.

To create a vegetarian version of typical Burmese condiments like *balachaung*, which has dried shrimp in it, we use a combination of ground roasted peanuts lightly fried with finely chopped onion, garlic and chilli with light soy sauce, lime juice, tamarind and honey.

In cafés and street food stalls of cities like Rangoon and Mandalay most fried dishes are cooked with an abundant use of peanut oil, which once cooked separates from the other ingredients and floats

on top of the dish. The idea is that the layer of oil preserves the underlying food from contamination by insects and airborne bacteria while the dishes sit in open, unheated pots for hours at a time. Customers are not expected to consume the oil but are served with spoonfuls of the ingredients from underneath. If all this sounds rather unappetizing, don't worry: there are plenty of Burmese dishes that have more appeal to sensitive stomachs.

The Burmese love to snack and the streets and markets are lined with vendors selling local delicacies, from the ubiquitous breakfast noodle soup *mohinga* to pickled tea-leaf salad.

Tea shops are an institution in Burma, used as meeting places for friends, family and even business associates. As well as tea, they serve a variety of snacks like *hsi htamin*, yellow sticky rice topped with sesame seeds and shredded coconut, and *sanwin makein*, another sticky rice snack coloured yellow with lashings of turmeric and served sweetened with chunks of banana wrapped in steamed banana leaves, with a name that amusingly translates as 'turmeric unavoidable'.

Some of the highlights of Burmese cuisine are the fresh salad dishes known as *thoks* or sometimes *lethoks.* These are light, spicy salads made with raw vegetables or fruit tossed with lime juice, onions, roasted peanuts, chillies, bean sprouts, coconut and lemon grass. Traditionally Burmese meals were concluded with a dish called *lephet thok*, which as the name suggests is a salad-like concoction, in this case made with moistened young leaves of green tea combined with sesame seeds, fried peas and beans, fried garlic, peanuts, toasted coconut and ginger. The slimy appearance of this dish can be a little off-putting; however, if you can get over this, it is actually quite tasty. In affluent circles *lephet* is served from elegant lacquer boxes with each ingredient in separate compartments. Some very beautiful *lephet* salvers made for Burmese aristocrats can be found for sale in Burmese markets. The more common village style of presentation is a simple tin plate. *Lephet thok* is usually served with a cup of tea. In Rangoon we found a shop selling do-it-yourself *lephet thok* kits with all the ingredients in separate sealed plastic bags.

Garlic and ginger on sale at Bharmo market, upper Burma

BURMESE DHOUO

1 small pomelo or large
  grapefruit
large handful of shredded
  white cabbage
2 carrots, cut into julienne
  strips
½ red pepper, thinly sliced
handful of skinless peanuts

For the dressing
2 shallots, roughly chopped

1 garlic clove
2 red chillies,
  roughly chopped
1 tablespoon sweet soy sauce
2 tablespoons lime juice
1 teaspoon honey
1 tablespoon sunflower oil
1 lemon grass stick,
  thinly sliced
small handful of chopped
  coriander

Peel the pomelo and then cut away each segment from the
pith with a serrated knife. Place in a bowl with the sliced
cabbage, carrots and red pepper.

  To make the dressing, blend or pound the shallot, garlic
and chilli together until a paste forms. Stir in the remaining
ingredients and season to taste. Combine with the salad and
leave to stand in the fridge for 10 minutes.

  Meanwhile roughly chop the peanuts and dry roast in a
small hot pan until golden. Sprinkle over the chilled salad just
before serving.

This spicy, zesty salad
is traditionally made
with pomelo, a citrus
fruit rather like a big
grapefruit. If you are
lucky enough to have
a good Asian store
nearby, shop for the
real thing; otherwise
the humble grapefruit
is a good substitute.

Left **Fruit seller on a
bank of the Irrawaddy**

Rose-scented, iced coconut milk with chopped lychees is almost like a pudding in a glass.

Use the best coconut milk you can find (read the label: the only ingredients should be coconut and water). If you have a problem sourcing jaggery you can substitute agave syrup, or brown sugar dissolved in a little hot water.

LYCHEE AND ROSE COCONUT MILK

1 tablespoon jaggery
1 litre/1¾ pints coconut milk
rose water to taste
12 lychees, preferably fresh,
peeled, stoned and cut into
quarters
ice, to serve

Finely chop the jaggery and mix with a little boiling water, until it has dissolved.

Whisk together the coconut milk, 240ml/8fl oz water and the jaggery syrup and stir in rose water to taste.

Serve in tall glasses over ice and the chopped lychees.

It is hard to ignore the politics of this part of the world; even the name of the country is contentious. As this book is about food rather than politics, we have decided to use words like Burma, Burmese, Irrawaddy and Rangoon, because every friend we made while we were travelling and eating our way around the country told us they preferred these to the alternatives used by the government.

Right **Bagan pagodas**

KATEN JOSHI THICK RED LENTIL SOUP WITH ALL THE TRIMMINGS

450g/1lb red split lentils
1¾ litres/3 pints vegetable
　　stock
a medium bunch of
　　coriander, finely chopped
½ teaspoon cracked black
　　pepper
salt to taste
cooked white basmati rice,
　　to serve

Toppings
6 green chillies, finely sliced
　　and soaked in 3 tablespoons
　　white wine vinegar for at
　　least half an hour
3 medium red onions, sliced
　　and gently fried in oil until
　　caramelized
1 medium sweet potato,
　　peeled, diced and fried in
　　oil until crisp and golden
a couple of slices of day-old
　　bread, cubed and fried in
　　oil until crunchy
chopped coriander leaves
wedges of fresh lime

Wash the lentils until the water runs clear, place in a saucepan and cover with the stock. Bring to the boil and gently simmer until the lentils break down and the soup has a porridge-like consistency. If any foam rises to the surface, simply skim off with a slotted spoon and discard. Stir in the chopped coriander, black pepper and salt.

　　Place a scoop of rice in the bottom of a deep bowl, ladle over the soup and help yourself to as many toppings as you fancy. Finally, squeeze the lime wedges over the top.

Soup is big in Burma and served with every meal, even breakfast. The options are endless: simple sweet broths, bitter broths, sour tamarind soups or thick and tasty pulse soups.

　　After an early morning start, lentil soup served splashed on to rice, and topped with pickled green chillies, cubes of golden sweet potatoes, crunchy fried bread and caramelized onions, fortified us for the next stage of our journey.

　　Prepare the toppings while the soup is bubbling away. Serve in individual bowls placed in the centre of the table.

Katen Joshi thick red lentil soup with all the trimmings

MOHINGA BREAKFAST SOUP

1 medium onion,
    roughly chopped
4 garlic cloves
5cm/2in piece of ginger root,
    peeled and roughly chopped
4 tablespoons sunflower oil
1 flat teaspoon ground chilli
1 teaspoon turmeric
1.5 litres/2½ pints vegetable
    stock
2 small onions, cut into quarters
3 stalks lemon grass, thinly sliced
2 tablespoons ground rice, dry
    roasted in a small pan until
    golden and mixed with a little
    cold water to a thin cream-
    like consistency
2 tablespoons light soy sauce
a handful or two of thinly sliced
    spinach leaves (optional)
1–2 flat teaspoons cracked
    black pepper

thin rice noodles, cooked
    (approximately 275g/10oz
    when dry; follow the
    cooking instructions on
    the packet), to serve

Toppings
chopped coriander leaves
lemon wedges,
    at least one per person
hard-boiled eggs
    (usually one per person),
    cut into quarters
chilli flakes
5 spring onions, sliced
110g/4oz shredded fine
    green beans
thinly sliced garlic, as much
    or as little as you desire,
    fried in sunflower oil until
    crunchy and golden

Blend the roughly chopped onion, garlic and ginger together
until a paste forms.

Heat the oil in a saucepan and gently sauté the onion paste
for 10 minutes or so. Stir in the turmeric, ground chilli and
vegetable stock.

Add the quartered onions and sliced lemon grass, and gently
simmer for 20 minutes.

Stir in the ground rice cream, soy sauce, spinach and black
pepper to taste, simmer for a further 10 minutes and season
to taste.

To serve, place a handful of rice noodles in a deep bowl, ladle
soup over the top and add the toppings of your choice.

The national dish
and breakfast staple
mohinga is definitely
the most important
meal of the day. There
are many recipes and
regional differences,
and every family has
its favourite *mohinga*
street vendor. Before
the tasks of the day
begin, the whole family
shares this ubiquitous
fish noodle soup.
Thanks to a nine-day
religious festival when
it is auspicious to eat
only a vegetarian
diet, there is also a
vegetarian recipe.

Serve ladled into
bowls with all the
important garnishes –
which you can prepare
while the soup is
cooking – placed in the
centre of the table.

In Burma *mohinga* is
seasoned with lots of
cracked black pepper.
We suggest starting
with 1 teaspoon and
adding more to taste.
A handful or two of
spinach leaves also
makes a good addition.

**The entrance to a
pagoda in Bagan**

A *thoke* is essentially a salad to accompany one of Burma's many delicious soups. It is made from raw, boiled or preserved vegetables, tossed with a tamarind, chilli and pounded dried prawn dressing, and topped with sliced onion or crispy garlic. The pounded prawns add a salty flavour that we replace with light soy sauce.

GREEN BEANS AND NEW POTATO THOKE

350g/12oz cooked baby
  new potatoes
200g/7oz blanched fine
  green beans
5 shallots, thinly sliced
a handful of chopped
  mint leaves

For the dressing
2 tablespoons tamarind water
2 tablespoons light soy sauce
2 tablespoons sunflower oil
1 teaspoon runny honey
2 red chillies, finely chopped

Place the warm cooked new potatoes and blanched green beans in a bowl.

Whisk the dressing ingredients together, pour over the vegetables and combine until well coated with dressing. Sprinkle the sliced shallots and chopped mint over the top before serving.

A typical Burmese coconut curry, combining flavours from India, China and home.

Chilli oil is available in most good food shops, or you can make your own by mixing chilli flakes to taste with oil.

AUBERGINE, PUMPKIN AND SHITAKE MUSHROOM CURRY

2 medium red onions,
   roughly chopped
4 garlic cloves, peeled
5cm/2in piece of ginger
   root, peeled and roughly
   chopped
4 tablespoons sunflower oil
½ teaspoon turmeric
1 teaspoon cayenne
2 teaspoons ground cumin
1 teaspoon ground coriander
2 teaspoons garam masala
1 cinnamon stick
2 bay leaves
450g/1lb cubed pumpkin
6 baby aubergines or
   1 medium aubergine, cubed

225g/8oz tinned chickpeas
10 shitake mushrooms,
   quartered
vegetable stock
2 tablespoons chickpea flour
   or ground rice
300ml/10floz coconut milk
1 tablespoons light soy sauce
flat rice noodles, to serve

To garnish
lemon wedges
chopped coriander leaves
thinly sliced shallots,
   dry- fried until crunchy
   and golden
chilli oil

Blend the onion, garlic and ginger together until a paste forms.

Heat the oil in a wok. When hot, add the onion paste, stir-fry for 5 minutes and then stir in the spices.

Add the pumpkin and aubergine, sprinkle a little salt on them to prevent the aubergine absorbing all the oil, and stir until well coated with the spices.

Add the chickpeas, shitake mushrooms and enough stock to nearly cover the vegetables. Simmer until the vegetables are just soft.

Mix the chickpea flour with a little water (to make a thick cream-like consistency) and stir into the curry, along with the coconut milk and soy sauce. Simmer for a further 5 minutes.

Serve with rice noodles, topped with garnishes of your choice.

A woman smoking a hand-rolled cigar with built-in coconut shell ashtray in Bagan

SESAME RICE

1 litre/1¾ pints cooked
  brown or white basmati
  rice (measured in a
  measuring jug)
3 tablespoons sunflower oil
2 medium onions, thinly sliced
2 garlic cloves, crushed
7 radishes, cut into cubes
2 carrots, cut into
  julienne strips
1 baby cucumber,
  cut into cubes
1 tablespoon sesame seeds
1 tablespoon tahini
  or sesame paste
good shake of light soy sauce
good squeeze of lemon
chopped coriander leaves,
  to garnish

Heat the oil in a wok. When it is hot, add the onion and garlic,
stir-fry for a couple of minutes, then add the vegetables and
cook for a further few minutes.

Add the sesame seeds and cooked rice, and stir-fry until the
rice is really hot. Finally, stir in the tahini, soy sauce and
lemon juice.

Serve with a little extra tahini drizzled on top and garnished
with chopped coriander leaves.

Serve with steamed
green vegetables for
a light lunch or as an
accompaniment to any
meal. Although it is not
strictly authentic, we
like to use brown rice
for extra texture.

**An abundance of
goods on sale in
Bharmo market**

We enjoyed this tofu stir-fry for lunch after a morning spent roaming the Buddhist temples of Bhamo. This close to the Chinese border, local cuisine has a stronger Chinese influence.

Ingredients are added in quick succession, so have them all at hand, ready to go.

TOFU AND WATERCRESS STIR-FRY

1 level teaspoon dried
  chilli flakes
1 tablespoon lemon juice
1 tablespoon light soy sauce
1 teaspoon runny honey
3 tablespoons sunflower oil
2 garlic cloves, crushed
400g/14oz firm tofu,
  cut into cubes

½ head Chinese leaves, sliced
2 tablespoons sesame seeds
2 bunches of watercress,
  roughly chopped,
  stalks and all
200g/7oz bean sprouts
a small bunch of chives, sliced
  into 4cm/1½in lengths

Mix the chilli, lemon, soy sauce and honey and leave to stand for 15 minutes.

In a wok heat the oil. When hot, add the garlic and tofu, and fry until golden.

Add the Chinese leaves and sesame seeds, stir-fry for a couple of minutes, then pour in the lemon mixture.

Add the watercress, bean sprouts and half the chopped chives, and cook for a further couple of minutes. Serve hot from the wok (before the watercress has wilted too much), topped with the remaining chives.

A mobile street-snack seller in Katha town

A delicious street snack topped with chopped onion and a squeeze of lemon – the perfect in-between-meals pick-me-up.

YELLOW SPLIT PEA FRITTERS

MAKES ABOUT 24

225g/8oz yellow split peas, soaked overnight

2 medium onions, very finely chopped

2 red chillies, finely chopped

½ teaspoon turmeric

½ teaspoon paprika

a good handful of chopped coriander

½ teaspoon black pepper

salt to taste, oil for frying

To garnish

thinly sliced shallots or red onion, mixed with a little chopped coriander and red chilli

lemon, cut into wedges

Drain and rinse the soaked yellow split peas. Blend half until a smooth paste forms and roughly chop the remaining half so that they still retain some bite.

Combine the prepared yellow split peas with the remaining ingredients.

Scoop out a dessertspoon of the mixture, roll between your hands to form a ball and then flatten to make a thickish patty. Repeat until all the mixture is used up.

Fry the fritters in a wok, five at a time, until they are golden brown on both sides.

Drain the fritters on kitchen paper before serving piping hot, sprinkled with the onion garnish and a good squeeze of lemon.

Dip hot fritters into this spicy sauce or spoon it on to rice, soups and curries.

Yellow split pea fritters

SPICY DIPPING SAUCE

2 garlic cloves, crushed

1 teaspoon grated ginger root

2 tablespoons tomato purée

1 tablespoon honey

4 tablespoons light soy sauce

½ teaspoon chilli flakes

Combine the garlic and ginger with the tomato purée. Stir in the honey, light soy sauce and chilli flakes.

Chile

TREKKING FROM THE ATACAMA
DESERT TO THE ANDES

Pages 62–63 **Panorama in the high Andes**
Below **Valle de la Luna**

As our lungs gasped at the thin mountain air in search of oxygen, our brains began to hurt. At an altitude of nearly 5,000 metres there was not much oxygen to be had. Something we had always taken for granted had now become the most precious thing in life. Our guide, Chino, reassured us in his laid-back, confident way that all we had to do was take it easy, slow down, and everything would be OK. He was right. It took a long time but eventually we reached the summit of the pass, to be rewarded by a spectacular panoramic view of the Salar de Talar, a vast snow-white salt pan surrounded by ashen-grey peaks of extinct volcanoes. This experience of a *travesia* or crossing of the Andes between Chile and Argentina by way of ancient high-altitude Inca trade routes is one we will never forget. It was an epic journey through some of the wildest, most spectacular places on earth.

Our journey began in the Spanish colonial oasis town of San Pedro, built around a fine white-washed plaza of adobe houses, shaded by tall trees and a very picturesque seventeenth-century church. It is located in the Atacama Desert of northern Chile, an extraordinary landscape of huge volcanoes (some of them still active), hill-top pre-Columbian ruins, hot springs hidden in valleys of papyrus grass, craters of wind-sculptured rock formations, vast salt pans rimmed with mountains where pink flamingos gather to feast on tiny shrimps in saline pools, and geothermal fields of gurgling, hissing geysers. We explored the café life of San Pedro in search of recipes we would be able to use later on the trip, when we would be cooking for ourselves. As we would be travelling by a combination of driving and walking, we were able to take a good range of local ingredients to cook and pre-prepared food for the journey in the vehicle.

By the time we were climbing up to the edge of Salar de Talar, the wind chill had dropped to -15°C/5°F. Once over the pass, we found a spot sheltered from the wind, where the sun was strong enough to warm us up instantly – enough to enjoy a picnic lunch of *sopaipilla* (pumpkin bread) sandwiches, quinoa salad and mushroom ceviche.

From here we travelled all the way to the 4,900-metre/16,000-ft Abra de Acay pass, from where we descended into the moister climate of the Argentine Andes, where plains full of giant cacti are surrounded by snow-capped peaks.

FOOD IN CHILE

Trekking in the footsteps of the Spanish conquistador Diego de Almagro through the surreal lava landscape of the Atacama Desert at such high altitude called for hearty stews and carb-rich snacks. Luckily, Chilean food, with its thick soups, one-pot bean stews, lashings of bread and pastries, is the ultimate comfort food.

Indigenous vegetables such as peppers, tomatoes, potatoes, chilli, corn, avocado and squash are mixed with Spanish flavours: *pimentón* (smoked paprika), oregano and olives, which the conquistadors carried with them. Chilean wine also adds depth to recipes and is a welcome accompaniment at mealtimes.

Chilean food tends not to be spicy, but *pebre*, a chilli and herb salsa, is used liberally to up the temperature. As soon as you sit down to eat, bread and *pebre* will automatically appear; dolloped on to bread, it's a wonderful way to take the edge off your appetite while perusing the menu.

Fresh lime juice is used to marinate raw fish and vegetables in the South American speciality ceviche; the citrus juice literally cooks the fish without heat. Chileans love pumpkin. It even manages to make its way into simple unleavened bread, sold in street stalls and topped with *pebre* or sugar syrup.

We munched our way through fortifying salads made from the protein-rich South American quinoa seed and creamy avocado, mouth-burningly hot pastry empanadas filled with locally made feta-style cheese and sweet, creamy, iced banana milk to drink.

Clockwise from top left **Piedra del Molino pass; crossing the Andes** *travesia* **route; cacti in the Calchaquies Valley; Reserva Nacional Los Flamencos**

VEGETARIAN CHARQUICAN

450g/1lb peeled,
    cubed potatoes
450g/1lb peeled, deseeded,
    cubed pumpkin
4 carrots, cubed
butter
olive oil
black pepper

For the pino
4 tablespoons olive oil
2 medium red onions, diced
2 garlic cloves, crushed
1 medium red pepper, diced
200g/7oz fine green beans,
    sliced into 1cm/½in pieces

110g/4oz frozen corn
1 heaped teaspoon
    ground cumin
1 teaspoon *pimentón*
½ teaspoon chilli flakes
1 heaped tablespoon
    chopped oregano leaves
3 medium tomatoes, diced
handful of chopped
    coriander

To serve
fried eggs
handful of chopped flat-leaf
    parsley
sliced spring onions

Simmer the potatoes, pumpkin and carrots in salted water
until soft, drain and then mash together with a knob of butter,
a drizzle of olive oil and plenty of ground black pepper, until
broken down but with chunky bits, not smooth.

Fry the red onion, garlic and red pepper in olive oil until
caramelized. Add the chopped beans and corn, and sauté for a
further few minutes.

Stir in the cumin, paprika, chilli and oregano until the
vegetables are coated in the spices. Add the diced tomato
and salt to taste. Gently simmer until the tomatoes are soft
and reduced.

Stir into the mashed potato, pumpkin and carrot, along
with the chopped coriander. Serve in individual portions,
topped with a fried egg and with chopped parsley and sliced
spring onions sprinkled on top.

Mashed pumpkin
and potato mixed
with a spicy *pino*
sauce, topped with
a fried egg, made
a typical warming
Chilean winter
dish. *Charquican* is
traditionally made with
dried llama meat, but
our trek cooks kindly
taught us how to make
a vegetarian version.

**High altitude trek in
the Poma Valley on
the Argentinian side.**

68

One taste of these pastry parcels stuffed with feta cheese, olives, raisins and chopped chives and we are instantly transported back to the surreal landscape of the Atacama. Empanadas are inseparable from *pebre* (see page 73) mixed with diced plum tomatoes. They can be fried in olive oil or baked in the oven; we prefer the easier option of baking, which is also much lighter on the waistline.

CHEESE, OLIVE AND RAISIN EMPANADAS

MAKES ABOUT 24

For the pastry
300g/10oz plain flour
1 egg yolk (retain the white and lightly whisk until frothy)
110g/4oz melted butter
180ml/6fl oz whole milk
½ teaspoon salt

For the filling
225g/8oz feta cheese, crumbled
handful of green olives, sliced
small handful of raisins
ground cumin
pepper
small handful of chives, chopped
pebre mixed with diced plum tomatoes to taste, to serve

Preheat the oven to 200°C/400°F/gas mark 6.

Combine all the pastry ingredients together in a bowl until a dough has formed. Leave to rest for 10 minutes.

Roll out the pastry on a floured surface and cut into 10cm/4in discs.

In the centre of each pastry disc place a little feta cheese, a few olive slices and raisins with a pinch of ground cumin, black pepper and chopped chives.

Brush whisked egg white around the edge of each empanada, fold in half, press the edges together and crimp with a fork. Brush the top with a little egg white.

Bake them in the preheated oven for 15 minutes or so, until they are golden.

Serve while still hot, dipped in *pebre* and plum tomato salsa.

This method of 'cooking' with lime juice works particularly well with mushrooms. In our camp the cook served mushroom ceviche topped with chopped avocado and tomatoes and with moreish sweet potato chips on the side.

We combine oyster and brown cap mushrooms, but you can substitute any mushrooms of your choice.

MUSHROOM CEVICHE

juice of 5 large limes
2 tablespoons avocado
    or olive oil
2 hot red chillies,
    thinly sliced
300g/10oz oyster mushrooms,
    roughly chopped
½ small red onion,
    thinly sliced
½ medium green pepper,
    thinly sliced
handful of chopped
    coriander

To serve
2 small, ripe avocados and 10
    cherry tomatoes, chopped
    and tossed with a good
    squeeze of lime juice and
    seasoning to taste
sweet potato slices fried
    in olive oil until golden
    (optional)

Whisk the lime juice, avocado oil and chilli together and season to taste. Gently combine with the mushrooms, red onion, pepper and chopped coriander, making sure all the vegetables are coated. Add seasoning to taste. Cover with cling film and chill in the fridge for 45 minutes.

Serve on a flat dish topped with the chopped avocado and cherry tomato salsa. Add fried sweet potato slices if desired.

Left **Mushroom ceviche**

Right **View from hotel in San Pedro**

CHILEAN TREKKERS' BREAKFAST

PER PERSON
2 slices hot buttered toast
1 large ripe avocado, sliced
2 eggs, fried in olive oil
a small handful of crumbled feta cheese
pebre

On the hot buttered toast lay the avocado slices, followed by fried eggs, crumbled feta cheese and black pepper. Top with a generous serving of *pebre*.

With sleeping bags for arctic condiitons, hot showers, food cooked using the ingredients we had brought with us from Chile, and plenty of good Latin wine, we managed to make even a night under canvas in sub-zero temperatures in the middle of nowhere a pleasure. Even though the *travesia* was behind us, we still had a long journey to make through the Argentinean Andes to the charming hill town of Salta and then on to Buenos Aires. Back down at sea level the air felt like oxygen soup.

In the cold of the early morning, we nursed our mugs of steaming hot coffee and watched the sun rise. The breakfast bell rang and breakfast was served: toast topped with avocado slices, fried eggs, crumbled feta cheese and *pebre* – a great way to start the day.

The silhouettes of trekkers in the Valle de la Luna in the Atacama Desert.

Pebre is so versatile: spread it on barbecued sweetcorn cobs, use it to spice up stews and soups or serve mixed with diced tomatoes with empanadas.

Medium-sized red chillies have lots of flavour as well as a good kick, but feel free to tailor the salsa to your preferred level of spiciness.

PEBRE: HERB AND CHILLI SALSA

a large handful of coriander
  leaves
a large handful of flat-leaf
  parsley
1 tablespoon oregano leaves
5 spring onions, sliced
2 garlic cloves, roughly
  chopped

chilli to taste, roughly
  chopped
3 tablespoons red wine
  vinegar
2 tablespoons lime juice
60ml/2fl oz olive oil

In a processor blend together all the ingredients except the oil until everything is finely chopped. Combine with the olive oil and season to taste.

Delectable creamy banana milk gave us a mid-afternoon injection of energy when spirits were flagging.

This recipe yields about 360ml/12fl oz of banana milk, enough for two thirsty people. Increase or decrease the quantities to make the desired amount, depending on how greedy you're feeling.

LECHE CON PLANTANO

1 large ripe banana
1 dessertspoon lime juice
honey to taste
240ml/8fl oz whole milk
60ml/2fl oz double cream
ice, to serve

Blend the banana, lime juice and honey to taste in a liquidizer until smooth. Add the milk and cream and blend until combined.

Serve poured over ice.

PORONTAS GRANADOS: CHILEAN BEAN STEW

4 tablespoons olive oil
1 medium onion, diced
1 red pepper, diced
2 leeks, sliced
1 scant dessertspoon
   pimentón
1 dessertspoon dried oregano
½ teaspoon ground black
   pepper
1 dessertspoon fine polenta
450g/1lb peeled, deseeded
   cubed pumpkin
3 corn cobs, cut into 2cm/
   ¾in slices

400g/14oz tin of haricot
   beans, drained and rinsed
400g/14oz tin of lima or
   butter beans, drained and
   rinsed
725ml/1¼ pints vegetable
   stock
handful of chopped basil
   leaves
salt to taste

To garnish
chopped coriander
Chilean salad (see opposite)

Heat the olive oil in a heavy-bottomed saucepan. When hot, add the onion, pepper and leeks, and sauté until soft.

Stir in the pimentón, oregano, pepper and polenta. Add the pumpkin, corn, drained beans and vegetable stock. Simmer until the pumpkin is soft (but not breaking down) and the sauce is thick and hearty, stirring occasionally to prevent sticking and adding a little more water if necessary.

Add the chopped basil and season to taste.

Serve in a bowl topped with Chilean salad and chopped coriander leaves.

Thick, hearty bean stew spiced with smoky *pimentón* makes a perfect comforting meal in a bowl.

Pimentón (smoked paprika) is available in sweet or spicy options. This recipe uses spicy *pimentón*, but you can use the sweeter option if you prefer.

Salt pans in the high Andes

CHILEAN SALAD

5 ripe plum tomatoes, sliced
1 medium red onion,
    thinly sliced

4 tablespoons olive oil
2 tablespoons lime juice
handful of chopped coriander

Arrange the tomatoes and red onion slices on a large plate.

Whisk the olive oil and lime juice together and season to taste. Pour evenly over the top of the salad and garnish with chopped coriander.

So simple and tasty, Chilean salad is used almost like a condiment. It's essential to use the very best ripe plum tomatoes.

SOPAIPILLA: PUMPKIN BREADS

MAKES ABOUT 24
250g/9oz peeled, deseeded,
    cubed pumpkin
6 tablespoons melted butter
325g/11oz plain flour

1 heaped teaspoon
    baking powder
oil for frying
pebre (see page 73), honey or
    maple syrup, to serve

Cook the cubed pumpkin in salted water until soft, drain (retaining the water) and mash with the butter until smooth.

Mix together the flour, baking powder and seasoning to taste, stir in the mashed pumpkin and a splash of the retained water, and knead together to make a dough. Leave to rest for 10 minutes.

Roll out the dough on a floured surface, until 6mm/¼in thick.

Cut into 8cm/3in circles and prick both sides with a fork to prevent the dough puffing up too much.

Either fry in oil in batches of four until golden on each side or bake in an oven preheated to 200°C/400°F/gas mark 6 for about 15 minutes.

Serve while still warm, topped with the sweet or savoury topping of your choice. They are also delicious served toasted the next day.

Street stalls selling fried mini pumpkin breads, smothered with savoury herb and chilli pebre or sweet sugar syrup, are a regular sight in Chile.

At home we bake the pumpkin breads, rather than frying them, and prefer a topping of honey or maple syrup rather than sugar syrup.

QUINOA SALAD

350g/12oz quinoa
725ml/1¼ pints vegetable
   stock
3 tablespoons olive oil
1 medium red onion, diced
1 medium sweet potato,
   peeled and diced
1 red pepper, diced
1 yellow pepper, diced
2 garlic cloves, crushed
1 teaspoon ground cumin
1 teaspoon paprika
2 medium avocados, diced
12 cherry tomatoes, diced
handful of chopped chives

For the dressing
2 tablespoons olive oil
1 tablespoon lime juice
salt and black pepper to taste

To garnish
a good handful of toasted
   pumpkin seeds
a handful of chopped
   coriander

Quinoa, a protein-rich, grain-like seed from an indigenous plant, is simmered in stock and served hot with stews or allowed to cool and used to make filling salads. Mixed with avocado, olives, peppers, tomato and toasted pumpkin seeds, it made a tasty movable feast for our trekkers' lunch.

Bring the quinoa and vegetable stock to the boil, cover the pan and simmer for 12 minutes. Turn off the heat and leave the covered pan to stand for a further 10 minutes. Fluff the cooked quinoa with a fork, to separate the grains, and leave to cool.

Meanwhile heat the olive oil and fry the onion, sweet potato, peppers and garlic until soft. Stir in the spices and allow to cool a little before combining with the quinoa, avocado, tomato and chopped chives.

Whisk the dressing ingredients together and carefully stir into the salad. Garnish with the toasted pumpkin seeds and chopped coriander leaves.

Quinoa salad

Cuba

IN SEARCH OF LIBERATED CUISINE
IN A CONVERTIBLE

We returned to Cuba after a gap of twenty years to find it
going through a new revolution, this time a culinary one.
Ingredients were in such short supply during the economic
decline that followed the collapse of the Soviet Union that the best
meal on offer in the state-run restaurants was a limp pizza base

with a smear of tomato paste and a slither of processed cheese. With revolutionary zeal Cubans rose to the challenge of shortages and began cultivating every spare plot of land to grow their own. Soon many Cubans who found they had a little spare produce began selling food cooked in their own homes to tourists on the black market. When these pop-up restaurants, known as *paladares*, were legalized they led the way in creating an adventurous style of fusion cooking, blending traditional Cuban dishes with other influences to create a new awakening in Cuban food, loosely referred to as Nueva Cocina Cubana.

Since then some Havana *paladares* like La Guarida have built international reputations for offering a winning combination of exciting menus of innovative cuisine in an atmosphere of retro Cuban cool. La Guarida has many imitators; new ones seem to be springing up all over the city almost daily.

In search of culinary treats beyond the capital, we hired an immaculate 1956 red Oldsmobile convertible and set off with the roof down in hot Caribbean sunshine on a road journey across the island.

First stop the fishing village of Cojimar, where we had a sensational seaside breakfast of *huevos habaneros* (eggs baked in a rich tomato sauce). There were no trendy *paladares* in Santa Clara, so we settled for the old Cuban classic of *moros y cristianos,* in a local café. It was a particularly good version, served with a fresh fried egg on top and livened up with plenty of home-made *mojo*, a sour orange and garlic sauce.

In the beautiful historic town of Trinidad we found *paladares* in magnificently restored mansions of sugar barons that rivalled any in Havana.

At a roadside stall next to a mask and snorkel hire shack on the shore of the Bay of Pigs, we stopped for a lunch of a spicy *garbanos* (vegetable stew) topped with a lively avocado and red onion salsa, with freshly baked crusty bread. The setting was wonderful: the crystal-clear Caribbean full of fish and coral on one side of the empty road and tropical jungle on the other. It was a perfect place for a glass of the local tipple, *coco loco* (a fresh coconut with half its water-filled interior replaced by rum), the ultimate organic cocktail, delicious and very Cuban.

Pages 78–79
Watching the world go by in the streets of Trinidad

Left **Our hired car – a 1956 red Oldsmobile convertible**

FOOD IN CUBA

Spanish, African and Caribbean cuisines, seasoned with Mexican, Chinese and French flavours, combine to create classic Cuban *criollo* cooking. Saffron, paprika, garlic, oregano, cinnamon and orange rub shoulders with black beans, olives, rice, peppers, tomatoes and corn. Produce might be limited but it is predominantly home grown, seasonal and organic.

Dense nutritious root vegetables such as yucca, potato and malanga provide energy-rich carbohydrates and are transformed into fritters or boiled and dressed with Cuban bitter orange, garlic and olive oil *mojo* sauce.

A sofrito of finely chopped onion, green pepper and garlic sautéed in olive oil is the foundation of many simple but tasty Cuban recipes. Spices and herbs are used modestly, but to great effect. Black beans and rice are still the mainstay of Cuban cuisine, served every which way, but traditionally is often best, with fried plantain and seasonal salad.

Peso stalls selling favourites such as croquettes, empanadas, mixto sandwiches and pizza are the perfect pit stop for a quick snack, but the stall with the longest queue is guaranteed to be for ice cream. Any time, day or night, Cubans' passion for this creamy delicacy is rivalled only by their love of rum and cigars. Hang out in the *casa* with a cup of home-grown café Cubana, espresso coffee sweetened with demerara sugar as it is brewed to give a deliciously smooth, sweet finish – perfect to dip buttered Cuban bread or sweet puff pastry *pastelitos* into.

In the bars classic Cuban rum-based cocktails such as the famous lime mojito or icy daiquiri are a great way to while away the evening, and around midnight *medianoche* (toasted sandwiches) are served to late-night revellers.

By the late evening the streets are teeming with families and friends enjoying the simple sounds of an acoustic guitar, a game of dominos and a glass of pure Cuban unadulterated rum.

Clockwise from top **A peso stall in Trinidad; pavement tacos; chillies on bike**

CARAMELIZED RUM AND COCONUT PINA ASADAS

1 medium pineapple
2 tablespoons unsalted butter
4 tablespoons dark rum
juice of a lime
½ teaspoon ground cinnamon

3 tablespoons demerara sugar
  or honey
a large handful of grated
  fresh coconut (wide grate)
ice cream, to serve

Peel the pineapple, making sure all the eyes are removed, and cut into thickish slices. Spear the slices with a fork and place in a flat dish.

Melt the butter in a small saucepan on a low heat, add the rum, lime, cinnamon and sugar, and stir together until the sugar has dissolved. Pour over the prepared pineapple and leave to stand for 15 minutes or so.

Sprinkle the pineapple slices with grated fresh coconut and grill, barbecue, griddle or fry until caramelized. Brush any remaining marinade on top of the pineapple slices, then turn and caramelize the remaining side.

Serve with a generous scoop of your favourite ice cream.

CLASSIC MOJITO

PER GLASS
30ml/1fl oz lime juice
1 tablespoon sugar syrup (see right)
small handful of fresh mint
55ml/2fl oz light Havana Club rum

a handful of ice, soda water

To garnish
mint leaves, a wedge of lime

Pour the lime juice and sugar syrup into a sturdy highball glass. Add a small handful of fresh mint and muddle or mash to release the flavour from the mint leaves. Add the rum, stir to lift the mint leaves, then add a handful of ice and top with soda water. Garnish with mint leaves and a wedge of lime.

On a balmy Caribbean evening, with the sound of waves crashing on the Malecon, we were introduced to the pleasures of pineapple caramelized with rum and fresh coconut served with ice cream.

Cuba's national drink and Ernest Hemingway's favourite tipple (his handwritten testament to this is still visible on the walls of La Bodeguita del Medio bar) is available anytime, anywhere. It is a classic highball of fresh lime, sugar syrup, whole mint, soda water and the best Cuban light rum.

To make sugar syrup, combine equal quantities of golden caster sugar and water in a small pan. Gently warm the pan until the sugar has dissolved. Allow to cool before serving.

View over the old quarter of Trinidad

SWEETCORN AND CARAMELIZED ONION TORTILLA DE PAPA

2 medium waxy potatoes,
    peeled and cut into quarters
2 tablespoons olive oil
2 tablespoons salted butter
1 large onion, thinly sliced
2 garlic cloves, finely chopped
a small handful of chopped
    thyme leaves
½ teaspoon paprika
¼ teaspoon ground cinnamon
6 large free-range eggs
a splash of whole milk/single cream
a small handful of flat-leaf
    parsley, finely chopped
55g/2oz grated Manchego or
    mature Cheddar cheese
110g/4oz sweetcorn kernels,
    fresh or frozen

Serve piping hot straight from the pan or allow to cool and cut into bite-size pieces to make tapas. Either way, tortilla is a regular Cuban favourite.

Cook the potatoes in salted water until nearly cooked but not completely soft. Drain and allow to cool for long enough for you to be able to handle them and cut into thin slices.

In a non-stick frying pan (approximately 25cm/10in), heat the olive oil and butter. When hot, add the onion, garlic and thyme. Lower the heat to a minimum, cover the pan and gently sauté until the onion is caramelized. Stir in the paprika and cinnamon.

Whisk the eggs with a splash of milk and season to taste. Add the sliced potato, parsley, grated cheese, sweetcorn and caramelized onion.

Return the frying pan to the stove, add a splash of olive oil and when hot add the egg mixture (spreading the potato, sweetcorn and onion evenly across the bottom). Cook on a medium heat until the tortilla is brown and coming away from the edges of the pan. Shake occasionally to prevent sticking.

Now for the brave part: time to turn the tortilla. It's easy, so don't worry! Remove the pan from the heat (allow to cool a little), place a plate over the frying pan, turn the tortilla on to the plate and then carefully slide it back into the pan. Fry the tortilla until brown and set in the middle. Alternatively, cook in a cast iron pan and place under a heated grill to cook the top.

Remove the pan from the heat and allow the tortilla to sit for 5 minutes before turning out on to a serving plate.

Chickpeas simmered with a Cuban sofrito of diced onion, green pepper and garlic, with the classic Galician spice combination of smoky pimentón and golden saffron strands. Serve with a simple avocado and red onion salsa, crusty bread and a sea view!

GARBANOS STEW

3 tablespoons olive oil
1 medium red onion, diced
½ medium green pepper, finely chopped
4 garlic cloves, finely chopped
1 jalapeño chilli pepper, thinly sliced
¾ teaspoon *pimentón*
¾ teaspoon ground cumin
10 cherry tomatoes, diced
60ml/2fl oz red wine
2 medium potatoes, peeled and diced

2 celery sticks, diced
1 small red pepper, diced
1½ tins (400g/14oz size) of chickpeas, drained and rinsed
3 bay leaves
heaped tablespoon chopped oregano leaves
360ml/12fl oz vegetable stock
½ teaspoon saffron

For the salsa garnish
2 large ripe avocados, diced
½ small red onion, diced
lime juice and salt to taste

Heat the olive oil and sauté the onion and green pepper until translucent. Add the garlic and jalapeño and sauté until soft.

Stir in the *pimentón* and ground cumin, followed by the chopped cherry tomatoes. When the tomatoes start to break down, add the red wine and simmer until the wine has reduced a little.

Add the remaining ingredients and simmer until the vegetables are nice and soft and the sauce is thick and rich. Season with salt and freshly ground black pepper to taste.

Mix the salsa ingredients. Ladle the stew into bowls and top with the salsa.

A fruit seller in the central market, Havana

HUEVOS HABANEROS: EGGS FROM HAVANA

SERVES 2

3 tablespoons olive oil
½ medium red onion,
   finely chopped
½ small green pepper,
   finely chopped
2 garlic cloves, crushed
½ teaspoon ground cumin
½ teaspoon ground cinnamon
180ml/4fl oz tinned chopped
   plum tomatoes

25g/1oz pimiento, diced
1 tablespoon dry sherry
   or white wine
4 medium free-range eggs
butter

To garnish
finely chopped flat-leaf
   parsley
pimentón

Recent liberalizations in Cuba have allowed the *paladares* to expand in size and to source new ingredients like salad and vegetables, which are now in abundance, not just in Havana but also around the island. Much of this culinary revolution has concentrated on dishes that pander to the Cuban relish of meat and fish, both of which had been so hard to find in the 'Special Period'; however, we found plenty of vegetarian treats on the *paladares*' menus and at roadside stalls.

Huevos habaneros – eggs baked in a rich tomato sauce – is traditionally a breakfast dish, but also makes a satisfying lunch or supper.

This recipe is for two people. Multiply quantities depending on how many you are feeding and bake in small individual dishes or together in one big dish.

Pimiento (roasted red peppers) are available preserved in olive oil in jars.

Preheat the oven to 190°C/375°F/gas mark 5.

Heat the olive oil and sauté the onion, pepper and garlic until soft but not brown. Stir in the cumin and cinnamon, followed by the tomatoes, pimiento and sherry. Simmer until the sauce is thick and rich, and season to taste.

Spoon the sauce into a baking dish (approximately 15cm/6in) or two individual dishes and carefully break the eggs on top (if you don't feel confident, break the eggs on to a saucer first and then slide on top). Season the eggs and liberally dot with butter.

Bake in the preheated oven for 15 minutes, after which the whites should be bubbling and cooked through. Sprinkle with a little finely chopped parsley and *pimentón*. Serve immediately with chunks of crusty bread.

Left **Grocery store in Trinidad**

Right **Huevos habaneros**

MOROS Y CRISTIANOS

4 tablespoons olive oil
1 large red onion, diced
4 garlic cloves, finely chopped
1 large red pepper, diced
2 dessertspoons paprika
1 tablespoon ground cumin
1 generous tablespoon
   chopped fresh thyme
3 bay leaves
1 teaspoon chilli flakes
1 tablespoon tomato purée
2½ tins (400g/14oz size) of
   black beans, drained
   and rinsed
300ml/10fl oz vegetable stock
1½ tablespoons red wine or
   cider vinegar

long-grain white rice
   (approximately 350g/12oz,
   depending on appetite)

To garnish
finely chopped fresh flat-leaf
   parsley
a generous drizzle of olive oil

To serve
a simple salad of lettuce leaves
   topped with thin slices
   of plum tomato, radish,
   avocado and red onion,
   dressed with seasoned olive
   oil and lime juice
fried plantain slices

Heat the olive oil and sauté the onion, garlic and red pepper until soft but not brown. Add the paprika, ground cumin, thyme, bay leaves and chilli flakes, cook for a couple of minutes and then stir in the tomato purée.

Add the beans and gradually stir in the vegetable stock. Simmer on a low heat until the stock has reduced by half, and mash the beans until they start to break down.

Add the red wine vinegar and season to taste with salt and freshly ground black pepper. Simmer for a further few minutes, and then serve either on top of or combined with cooked white long-grain rice. Garnish with finely chopped parsley and a generous drizzle of olive oil. Serve the simple salad and fried alongside.

Literally translated as Moors and Christians, this dish of black beans and white rice is still the mainstay of Cuban cuisine. The beans and the rice are either served separately or combined, usually with a simple fresh salad and fried plantain. Or you can enjoy them as we did, mixed together, topped with a fried egg and doused with zesty *mojo* sauce (see page 94).

A typically opulent Cuban *paladar*

From the ground floor the entrance to the Paladar La Guarida looked like the film set of a post-apocalyptic disaster film. Things didn't improve much on the first floor, where washing was hanging out to dry above a gang of boys engrossed in a noisy makeshift football match using a baseball. The crumbling, once ornate, sweeping stairway led us on upwards from the peeling Italianate loggia to a modest doorway. There at last was a sign that confirmed that, far from making a horrible mistake, we had in fact found the location of the most talked-about culinary experience in Havana.

Just the other side of the door was one of the most seductively eclectic and poetically evocative restaurants in the world, a winning combination of antique colonial furniture, English dinner services, Venetian glassware, Catholic effigies, art deco lamps and contemporary Cuban art. The customers looked as cool as the décor. Even better, the food was sensational. That statement would have been unthinkable anywhere in Cuba when we came here twenty years ago for our first book. A lot has changed since then – but not too much, thankfully, and as far as food is concerned all of it for the better.

PUFF PASTRY PASTELITOS

MAKES 6
375g/13oz ready-rolled
   puff pastry

For the cheese picadillo
2 tablespoons olive oil
½ medium red onion, diced
2 garlic cloves, crushed
60ml/2fl oz tinned chopped
   plum tomatoes
4 cherry tomatoes, diced
1 tablespoon red wine

1 tablespoon chopped
   oregano leaves
a handful of black olives,
   finely chopped
a handful of raisins
25g/1oz grated Manchego or
   strong Cheddar cheese

For the sweet glaze
½ teaspoon honey dissolved
   in 1 teaspoon warm water

Preheat the oven to 190°F/375°C/gas mark 5.

Heat the olive oil and sauté the onion and garlic until translucent. Add the tomatoes, red wine and oregano and simmer until the sauce has thickened.

Remove the pan from the heat and stir in the chopped olives, raisins and cheese. Season to taste.

Cut the puff pastry into twelve equal squares (approximately 8cm/3in square). Place a generous tablespoon of the picadillo in the centre of six squares, moisten the edges with water and place the remaining squares on top. Press the edges together, crimp with a fork and brush with the sweet glaze.

Place on a non-stick baking tray and bake in the preheated oven for 15 minutes, after which the pies should be puffed up, golden brown and ready to eat.

Puff pastry pies stuffed with a choice of savoury or sweet fillings are classic Cuban street food. Cheese picadillo makes a favourite lunch stuffing, or, for the sweet toothed, guava jam with sweetened cream cheese. Whatever the filling, a sweet glaze is a prerequisite.

For an easy life, buy ready-rolled sheets of puff pastry.

To make sweet *pastelitos*, instead of picadillo substitute a dessertspoon of cream cheese mixed with a little honey and a dessertspoon of jam, marmalade, cooked fruit or fruit cheese.

Paella with a twist! The paella rice is cooked with beer and saffron for that authentic Cuban flavour.

Serve topped with lashings of grated Manchego cheese, olive oil and chilli flakes and a side serving of steamed broccoli, asparagus or spinach dressed with *mojo* sauce (see page 94).

Artichoke hearts and pimiento (roasted red peppers) can be bought marinated in olive oil in jars.

Puff pastry *pastelitos*

TRINIDAD SAFFRON AND ARTICHOKE RICE

5 tablespoons olive oil
1 medium onion, diced
1 small green pepper, diced
1 small red pepper, diced
4 garlic cloves, finely chopped
½–1 teaspoon chilli flakes
1 flat teaspoon *pimentón*
2 plum tomatoes, diced
2 carrots, diced
300g/11oz paella or long-grain white rice
480ml/16fl oz light beer
240ml/8fl oz vegetable stock
½ teaspoon saffron
4 bay leaves
½ teaspoon dried oregano

a handful of finely chopped flat-leaf parsley
110g/4oz frozen peas
1 tin (400g/14oz size) of butter beans, drained and rinsed
6 marinated artichoke hearts, cut into quarters
50g/2oz pitted black olives, cut in half
50g/2oz pimiento, sliced

To garnish
A generous drizzle of olive oil
grated Manchego or Parmesan cheese
finely chopped parsley
chilli flakes

In a heavy-bottomed pan heat the olive oil. When hot, sauté the onion, diced peppers and garlic until soft.

Stir in the chilli flakes and *pimentón*, followed by the diced plum tomatoes and carrots.

Add the rice and combine with the onion spice mixture until well coated. Add the beer, vegetable stock, saffron, bay leaves, oregano and parsley. Cover the pan and gently simmer until the rice is nearly cooked and the liquid reduced (stirring the rice from time to time to prevent sticking).

Stir in the peas, butter beans, artichoke hearts, black olives and pimiento. Season to taste and simmer until the vegetables are heated through.

Serve with a generous drizzle of olive oil, grated cheese, parsley and chilli flakes to taste.

ZESTY MOJO SAUCE

180ml/6fl oz Seville orange
  juice or 120ml/4fl oz orange
  juice, 30ml/1fl oz lime juice
  and 30ml/1fl oz lemon juice
1 flat teaspoon sea salt
½ teaspoon crushed black
  peppercorns
½ teaspoon ground cumin

½ small onion, very finely
  chopped (optional)
60ml/2fl oz olive oil
8 garlic cloves, crushed
chopped oregano leaves
  (optional)
chopped coriander leaves
  (optional)

Combine the citrus juice, salt, black pepper, cumin and (if you want a thicker sauce) onion.

Heat the olive oil in a small saucepan. When hot, add the crushed garlic and sauté for a couple of minutes until soft but not brown.

Remove the pan from the heat and allow to cool for a few minutes before pouring in the citrus mix (stand back a little, just in case it spits). Return to the heat and bring to the boil; then remove from the heat once more and allow to cool, when you can add the herbs if you wish.

The *mojo* sauce can be stored in an airtight container in the fridge for a few days.

BEETROOT, PUMPKIN AND AVOCADO SALAD WITH MOJO SAUCE

Layer slices of cooked beetroot (make sure it is unadulterated, with no added vinegar), pumpkin or sweet potato boiled until soft, avocado and grapes on a bed of roughly chopped cos lettuce leaves. Top with finely sliced red onion and *mojo* sauce to taste. Garnish with chopped fresh coriander leaves.

Clockwise from top left **Mural of Fidel; pizza menu; vintage car in old Havana; sandwich stall in Trinidad; hole-in-the-wall snack bar**

Mojo sauce, originally from the Canary Islands, is one of Cuba's most adaptable signature recipes. It adds zest to black beans or cooked cassava, makes an exciting marinade and is the perfect dipping sauce for malanga fritters and grilled Cuban sandwiches.

There are many recipes for *mojo*, often depending on what the sauce is being used for that day, but its essential ingredients are Cuban bitter Seville oranges, garlic, a little cumin, black pepper and salt. For vegetarian dishes olive oil is also an important addition, as is finely chopped onion for a dip or condiment. The sauce is also delicious with chopped fresh oregano or coriander leaves stirred into it.

When Seville oranges are out of season, simply mix orange juice with lemon and lime. It's not quite the same but a good second best.

OFERTA HOY

Pizza "Queso $ 6.00   Pizza "Queso $ 30.00
Pizza "Jamón $ 10.00   Pizza "Jamón $ 50.00
Pizza "Domicilio   Pizza "Chorizo $ 45.00
Pizza
Batidos sabores de HOY
Guayaba $ 3.00
Mango $ 3.00

PAN CON
MINUTA $5.00

Japan

ANCIENT GARDENS BY BULLET TRAIN

Pages 96–97 **An avenue of** *torii* **gates at the Fushimi-Inari Taisha shrine near Kyoto**

Below, clockwise from top left **Hoshinoya** *ryokan*, **Arashiyama; Kiyomizu Temple, Kyoto, in the rain; bamboo forest**

One of the greatest joys of travel is those unexpected perfect moments that come out of nowhere – experiences that make the whole journey worthwhile and provide an everlasting memory. Travelling in Japan offered us so many that we lost count. The best one included torrential rain, and anywhere that can deliver a moment of pure joy in pouring rain has to have a lot to offer – as Japan certainly does. It was the only country in Asia we had not been to before, and travelling there was like discovering a secret new world that no one had ever told us about. On the surface many things seemed familiar but this was an illusion. Travelling anywhere without speaking the local language is always a challenge but when it's somewhere without a Roman alphabet it's twice as hard. Travelling in Japan, however, these disadvantages became a joy, as they forced us to interact with people along the way.

Armed with rail passes and an English timetable, and aiming to stay in traditional inns or *ryokans* everywhere we went, we set off on what felt like a real adventure. *Shinkansen* (bullet trains) took us at incredible speeds between the main cities and connected seamlessly with more conventional express services to smaller rural towns, on a journey that took us from Tokyo across to Kanazawa, a charming provincial town located between the Japanese Alps and the Japan Sea, then west to Okayama on the Kibi Plain and finally via Kyoto to Mito and Senba Lake on the Pacific coast.

Every train was spotless, comfortable and on time. The ticket collectors and snack sellers bow three times to the passengers as they enter and leave each carriage. The whole trip went perfectly until flooding and destruction caused by the worst typhoon to hit Japan for a decade trapped us at Hoshinoya *ryokan*, deep in the leafy bamboo forest of the temple-rich Kyoto suburb Arashiyama.

There can be few places in the world better to be stuck in. We watched the rain fall like silver rods through golden maple leaves into the roaring river below, framed by the sliding rice paper and bamboo screen window of our wonderful room. Knowing that it was impossible to do anything except enjoy the delicious breakfast laid out on the table in front of us made it a moment of perfection.

FOOD IN JAPAN

Japanese recipes are not necessarily difficult but you do need to be prepared with the right ingredients. These days they are readily available from Asian stores, good supermarkets and specialist food shops. The delicate flavours of miso, shoyu and mirin form the basis of sauces and broths, with ginger and the pungent horseradish condiment wasabi providing some heat. Tofu, beans, seaweed, lotus root, mushrooms, squash, turnip, white radish and various different leaves are lightly simmered, steamed, grilled or fried to provide the correct balance of crunch and softness.

As far as eating was concerned, menus in Japanese were useless to us. Luckily most restaurants specialize in just one type of food, like sushi or tempura or tofu, and have either photographs or models of all the dishes they serve. In the cities we found enough people who spoke English to help us find out which of the dishes were vegetarian and we memorized what they were called and looked like in order to survive in the small towns and countryside. Vegetarian dishes are common, but purists need to watch out for the ubiquitous *dashi* (fish stock), an important ingredient in many Japanese dishes.

Simplicity is at the heart of the philosophy of Japanese cuisine. Fresh ingredients are served raw, lightly cooked or cured, with sauces often served separately, to maintain their integrity of taste.

Preparation is meticulous. Vegetables are cut into artistic bite-size pieces (just the right size for chopsticks), cooked to the exact level of crunchiness and beautifully displayed on lacquer or fine china serving dishes. A whole array of simple small dishes can constitute a meal. Sake is drunk throughout and on special occasions the principal guest starts the party by first drinking three cups in quick succession. Green tea always finishes the meal.

Left **A shinto shrine in Nara**

Far left **Tea pots in a Kanazawa garden tea shop**

Right **A bride in Koraku-en garden**

Curry arrived in Japan from India via England. The recipe has been added to over the years and evolved into a distinctive aromatic thick sauce, which is served over rice with different toppings.

The base to a Japanese curry is a roux; ready-made roux are sold in bars that look strangely like chocolate. At a tiny curry house in Okayama we were served a dish based on a home-made curry roux, topped with steamed vegetables – florets of cauliflower, broccoli, carrots, beans and courgettes. At home we also like to add fried tofu.

OKAYAMA VEGETABLE CURRY

5 tablespoons butter
2 medium onions, thinly sliced
3 garlic cloves, crushed
2.5cm/1in piece of ginger root, peeled and grated
1 large eating apple, grated
4 tablespoons plain flour
1 tablespoon mild curry powder

a pinch of cayenne pepper
1 tablespoon tomato purée
1 litre/1¾ pints vegetable stock
3 bay leaves
2 star anise
2 tablespoons shoyu
½ teaspoon black pepper
1 tablespoon garam masala
1 teaspoon honey

In a saucepan melt the butter, add the onion, garlic, ginger and apple, and sauté until caramelized.

Stir in the flour, curry powder and cayenne to make the roux base. Add the tomato purée and gradually stir in the stock until well combined.

Add the bay leaves, star anise, shoyu, pepper, garam masala and honey. Simmer until the sauce thickens and the oil returns. Season to taste.

Serve spooned over Japanese short-grain rice (see page 108), topped with steamed vegetables of your choice.

BUCKWHEAT NOODLES AND SPINACH WITH DIPPING SAUCE AND WASABI

450g/1lb *soba* buckwheat
noodles
5 spring onions, thinly sliced
1 sheet nori seaweed,
cut into thin 4cm/1½in-long
thin strips
1 dessertspoon black
sesame seeds

500g/1lb 2oz spinach
wasabi, to serve

For the dipping sauce
120ml/4fl oz shoyu or light
soy sauce
120ml/4fl oz mirin
240ml/8fl oz water

First make the dipping sauce. Place all the ingredients in a pan and bring to the boil. Boil rapidly for a couple of minutes and then reduce the heat and simmer for a further few minutes. Remove from the heat and pour into individual bowls, ready to serve with the noodles.

Cook the *soba* noodles as instructed on the packet, drain and thoroughly rinse in cold water to remove all traces of starch – the noodles should feel nice and elastic.

Wind the noodles into neat bonfire-shaped piles on individual plates. Sprinkle with half the spring onions, nori strips and black sesame seeds.

Plunge the spinach in salted boiling water until wilted, drain and then rinse with cold water. Place in a colander and press any excess water away. Slice the spinach into 2cm/¾in strips.

Place the spinach next to the noodles in as similar a shape as possible, and sprinkle with the remaining nori strips, spring onions and black sesame seeds. Finally, place ½ teaspoon of wasabi on each plate.

To eat, mix a little wasabi in the dipping sauce and then dip the noodles and spinach in the sauce until coated. Accompany with silken tofu topped with ginger and chives (see page 111) if you wish.

Right **Wasabi**
Far right **Buckwheat noodles and spinach with dipping sauce and wasabi**

On humid hot summer days street stalls in Tokyo sell the cooling dish of *soba* buckwheat noodles and lightly cooked spinach, served cold with shoyu and mirin dipping sauce mixed with wasabi. Serve accompanied by cool silken tofu simply garnished with grated ginger and chives.

Wasabi, a green horseradish paste, adds spice to Japanese dishes. Buy it ready mixed in a tube or powdered (simply mix the powder with a little water to make a paste). Use sparingly if you are not familiar with it, as it has quite a kick.

Crisp, thin nori seaweed sheets are most commonly used to make sushi.

Sweet, alcoholic mirin is an essential ingredient in Japanese cooking, used to balances the salty flavour of shoyu, a Japanese soy sauce.

MARINATED TOFU WITH SESAME, WATERCRESS AND POACHED QUAILS' EGGS

560g/1 lb 4 oz firm tofu
plain flour
4 tablespoons sunflower oil
2 handfuls of watercress,
    chopped through
4 lightly poached quails' eggs

Marinade
4 garlic cloves, sliced
5 spring onions
4 tablespoons each of mirin,
    sake and shoyu or light soy
    sauce
120ml/4fl oz mirin
240ml/8fl oz water

Drain the tofu and pat dry with kitchen paper. Cut into quarters, then cut each quarter lengthwise and coat with plain flour.

Heat the oil in a wok and fry the tofu until it is golden brown on both sides. Remove from the pan and set to one side while you make the marinade.

Put the garlic into the wok and fry until crunchy. Add the rest of the marinade ingredients and simmer for a couple of minutes.

Place the tofu in individual shallow bowls, pour over the marinade, scatter with chopped watercress and top with the poached eggs.

In the hot springs of Japan, eggs are poached in the steamy sulphurous waters; the pungent soft eggs are then served with tofu.

If you have difficulty finding quails' eggs, you can substitute free-range hens' eggs or, alternatively, slices of avocado.

Below left Raked Zen garden at Hoshinoya in Arashiyama

Below right Wild deer roaming freely at Todai-ji Nandaimon gate in Nara

Breakfast traditionally consists of miso soup, rice and pickles. Lunch may be a steaming bowl of *soba* noodle broth, a spiced curry at one of Japan's popular curry restaurants or one of the many different *bento* lunch boxes on offer. Sushi restaurants range from simple to very smart, with prices to match. For a good-value evening meal locals head to the *izakaya*, a bustling Japanese pub serving local beer and sake, instantly recognizable by a red lantern at the door. Tofu restaurants, tempura restaurants, *sukiyaki* restaurants – there are endless places to enjoy every conceivable Japanese speciality.

MISO-SIMMERED AUBERGINE

8 dried shitake mushrooms,
    soaked in 120ml/4fl oz hot
    water until soft
3 tablespoons sesame oil
8 baby aubergines, cut into
    quarters lengthwise
3 tablespoons red miso
180ml/6fl oz hot vegetable
    stock

2 carrots, cut into
    julienne strips
2 tablespoons mirin
2 tablespoons shoyu
    or light soy sauce
1 dessertspoon honey
125g/5oz mangetouts
1 baby leek or 4 spring
    onions, shredded, to serve

Strain the shitake mushrooms and cut them into quarters.
Reserve the drained liquid,

Heat the sesame oil in a wok, add the aubergines, sprinkle
with salt and stir-fry until soft.

Dissolve the miso in the hot vegetable stock and add 5
tablespoons of the retained shitake water (avoiding any grit in
the bottom of bowl). Pour over the aubergines and add the
quartered mushrooms and the carrot strips. Simmer for 5 minutes.

Add the mirin, shoyu and honey, followed by the
mangetouts. Simmer for a couple of minutes until al dente.

Serve garnished with shredded leek, with sticky rice (see
page 108) on the side.

There is still a strong tradition of *shojin ryori* at some Buddhist temples in Japan: vegan recipes are cooked at mealtimes and available to all. We sampled aubergine simmered in a flavoursome stock served with sticky rice.

Left **Gardeners on a tea break in Kenroku-en garden**

Miso soup and rice are considered the foundation to every meal. They start the day at breakfast time, served simply with crisp vegetable pickles, and with the addition of side dishes become a feast at suppertime.

Miso, a thick paste made from fermented soya beans and grain, comes in three different types: strong-flavoured red, sweet white and medium, which is somewhere in between the two. We tend to use medium, but experiment to find which you prefer.

At home we often add more vegetables to this basic recipe to make a quick, nutritious and filling meal.

MISO SOUP AND RICE

5g/¼oz wakame seaweed
1½ litres/2½ pints vegetable stock
3 tablespoons medium miso

225g/8oz silken tofu, cut into cubes
4 spring onions, finely chopped, to serve

Soak the wakame in hot water for a few minutes until reconstituted. Drain and cut into bite-size pieces.

Pour the stock into a saucepan and bring to the boil. Thin the miso by combining a ladle of the hot stock with the miso in a separate bowl.

Lower the heat and add the thinned miso to the pan. Ensure you do not boil the miso.

Add the wakame and tofu, simmer for a couple of minutes and then serve sprinkled with chopped spring onion and with sticky rice (see page 108) on the side.

We also enjoy miso with:
grated ginger root
sliced shitake mushroom or wood ear mushrooms
endame beans (fresh soya beans)
broccoli, shredded carrot, pak choi

Koi carp at Kenroku-en

JAPANESE RICE

To achieve the perfect sticky rice, first thoroughly wash the rice until the water runs clear.

240ml/8fl oz of rice makes average portions for four or generous portions for three. To cook the rice, it is best to use slightly more water than rice. We use a measuring jug for good results – 240ml/8fl oz Japanese rice to 300ml/10fl oz cold water.

Place the washed rice in a heavy-bottomed pan and pour over the correct quantity of water. Bring to the boil, cover with a tight-fitting lid, then reduce the heat to the minimum and gently simmer for 12 minutes. Turn off the heat and leave to stand for a further 10 minutes. Don't be tempted to remove the lid at any point!

Gently fluff the rice with a rice spoon; the sticky rice will naturally clump together a little.

Rice is considered the foundation of cuisine in Japan and this is aptly reflected in the translation of the name for cooked rice: meal. Japanese rice is short grain and cooked so that it is just sticky enough to be eaten easily with chopsticks but still retains a little bite.

Rice and pickle go hand in hand in Japan. Barrels filled with pickles are displayed in food stores and 'try before you buy' is encouraged.

To preserve the pickle, vegetables are lightly salted and combined with the subtle flavours of sake or miso.

Ornamental bonsai tree in Koraku-en garden

MIXED VEGETABLE PICKLE

2 Chinese leaves, cut into bite-size cubes
2 red cabbage leaves, cut as above
1 carrot, cut into julienne strips
¼ kohl rabi or young turnip, cut into julienne strips
¼ cucumber, cut into fat julienne strips
fine sea salt
25g/1oz raisins, chopped
90ml/3fl oz sake (or 1 heaped teaspoon miso dissolved in 90ml/3fl oz warm water)

Place the prepared vegetables in a bowl and sprinkle with a good shake of sea salt. Stir well to ensure all the vegetables are coated in the salt. Set to one side for 10 minutes.

Knead the vegetables with your hands and squeeze out any excess liquid.

Place the vegetables in a clean bowl along with the chopped raisins and the sake.

Cover the vegetables with a plate (smaller than the bowl) and place a heavy weight on top. Leave to stand for 20 minutes. Tip into a sieve and drain away any excess liquid. The pickle is then ready to serve.

Most Japanese gardens are private affairs associated with palaces, temples or tea gardens. Some are in small courtyards bursting with carefully manicured foliage; others feature intricate systems of connecting streams, pools and water features or minimalist meditation spaces of raked gravel and carefully placed rocks. The three 'great gardens' of Japan, considered the most beautiful of all, are open to everyone. They are vast expanses of tamed nature and subtle topiary, designed and constructed in the grounds of medieval castles originally for the strolling pleasure of their imperious owners.

The three great gardens all have very similar names: Kenroku-en, Koraku-en and Kairaku-en (*en* obviously meaning garden). All of them were well worth visiting, but the real pleasures of the trip were the food, the people and the *ryokans*.

ROLL YOUR OWN SUSHI

SERVES 6

12 sheets nori seaweed, cut
  into quarters
shoyu or light soy sauce,
  served in individual bowls
wasabi
ginger root, peeled and grated

For the rice
4 tablespoons rice vinegar
6 teaspoons caster sugar
  (or to taste)
1 teaspoon salt
480ml/16fl oz Japanese rice,
  cooked as described on
  page 108

*Suggested fillings: take your pick
  or add your own*
avocado, cut into thin strips and
  dressed with lemon
carrots, cut into julienne strips
cucumber, cut into julienne strips
raw beetroot, cut into julienne
  strips
chives, cut into 4cm/1½in
  lengths
raw mushrooms, thinly sliced; try
  oyster and brown cap
marinated or deep-fried tofu, cut
  into strips
mustard and cress
plain egg omelette, cut into strips
pickled ginger
mayonnaise

A popular addition to *bento* lunch boxes or an appetizer with a glass of sake, sushi comes in many types and shapes. Pricey specialist restaurants serve exquisite sushi prepared by expert chefs, who have trained for years to learn the complex art of sushi making. Sushi rolling parties are also all the rage. All the ingredients are laid out on the centre of the table and guests help themselves. With a glass of beer to jolly things along, this is a great, relaxed way to enjoy sushi with friends.

Good sushi rice is imperative to the perfect sushi. It is a combination of warm sticky Japanese rice and sweetened, salted rice vinegar. Ready-mixed sushi rice vinegar is available, but we have included the recipe in case you find it hard to buy. The amount of sushi vinegar added to rice depends on personal taste. The recipe is for medium seasoning, but personalize to your own taste.

To make the sushi rice, gently warm the rice vinegar with the caster sugar and salt, and stir until dissolved. Place the cooked rice in a bowl, pour the sweetened vinegar evenly over the top and gently combine. Cover the bowl with a cloth and leave to stand for 10 minutes.

Place the rice, nori seaweed sheets and fillings of your choice in the centre of the table.

Provide each of your guests with a plate and spoon, a small bowl of shoyu, a little wasabi, some grated ginger root and these basic instructions: place a sheet of nori seaweed on your hand, spread a level tablespoon of rice over the top, add wasabi and grated ginger to taste and top with a little of the selected filling. Roll into a tight cone shape and finally dip into shoyu before each bite. Accompany with warm sake and beer. Happy rolling!

Here soft, silken tofu is simply prepared, topped with shisho leaves, grated ginger and chopped chives, to maximize the subtle taste and texture of the tofu.

Tofu is a staple ingredient in Japan. It comes in two types: soft silken tofu, best used uncooked, and firm tofu, where the bean curd is pressed to create a firmer texture, more suitable for cooking.

Shiso leaves are a common flavouring in Japan. You can substitute a mix of basil and mint leaves if they are unavailable.

SILKEN TOFU WITH GINGER AND CHIVES

SERVES 4

560g/1lb 4oz silken tofu	*For the dipping sauce*
a thumb-sized piece of ginger root, peeled and grated	60ml/2fl oz shoyu or light soy sauce
2 tablespoons chopped chives	2 tablespoons mirin
2 tablespoons chopped shiso or mixed basil and mint leaves	1 tablespoon sake
	½ teaspoon brown sugar

Drain the tofu and carefully pat dry with kitchen paper. Cut into oblong pieces and place in individual serving bowls.

Warm the shoyu, mirin, sake and sugar together until the sugar dissolves.

Place a serving of grated ginger on the tofu, artistically sprinkle chives and shiso leaves on top and finally drizzle the dipping sauce around the tofu.

Silken tofu with ginger and chives

Staying in up-country *ryokans* offered us an intimate experience of the elegant simplicity of the traditional Japanese way of life. The minimalist rooms have *tatami* (straw mat) flooring, *shoji* (sliding rice paper screens), futon-style beds and *yukata* (dressing gowns). The *ryokans* range from relatively modest family-run affairs to seriously opulent resorts. As soon as you arrive, you surrender your shoes for slippers that in turn are left outside your room. Bathing involves a good scrub in private before joining other guests in a communal wooden hot tub. At all the *ryokans* we stayed in, our hosts were happy to provide us with vegetarian versions of traditional local dishes and they were always delicious.

Clockwise from top left Zen temple garden in Kyoto; bamboo forest in Kairaku-en garden; deer among the stone lanterns at Kasuga Taisha shrine; Kanazawa tea house; Kanazawa garden

VEGETABLE AND UDON NOODLE BROTH

450g/1lb *udon* noodles
1.2 litres/2 pints vegetable
    stock
a thumb-sized piece of ginger
    root, peeled and shredded
5 dried shitake mushrooms,
    soaked in boiling water
    until soft and then
    thinly sliced
a medium head of broccoli,
    cut into small florets
2 carrots, cut into
    julienne strips
125g/4oz oyster mushrooms,
    sliced

a couple of handfuls of
    sliced spinach
225g/8oz tofu, cubed
3 tablespoons shoyu
    or light soy sauce
1½ tablespoons mirin
1½ tablespoons sesame oil

To serve
Nanami togarashi: chilli
    pepper ground with sesame
    seeds, ginger and seaweed
    (or, if you cannot find this
    spicy Japanese condiment,
    garnish with chilli flakes
    and sesame seeds)

Cook the *udon* noodles as instructed on the packet, drain and
divide between deep bowls.

Pour the vegetable stock into a saucepan. Add the shredded
ginger and prepared vegetables. Simmer until the vegetables
are soft but still retain a little bite.

Add the tofu, shoyu, mirin and sesame oil, and simmer for
a further couple of minutes. Ladle the broth over the noodles
and sprinkle with *nanami tagarashi* to taste.

Thick, chewy, *udon*
noodles served in a clear
broth make a comforting
and good-value supper.

Udon noodles are
sold fresh or frozen;
keep a handy packet in
the freezer for a quick,
satisfying meal.

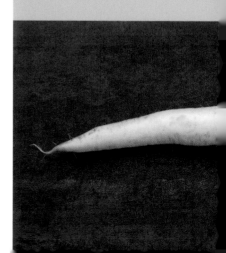

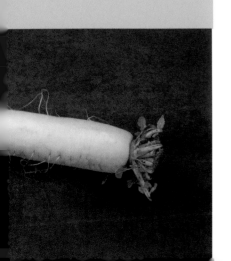

Crisp and light battered vegetables served with dipping sauce, grated ginger and mooli became our guilty pleasure when, mid-afternoon, supper seemed just too far away.

Almost any vegetable combination makes great tempura. Just make sure the vegetables are completely dry before dipping them into the batter.

For perfect tempura, the batter mixture must be icy cold and handled as little as possible. Place water in the icebox with a handful of ice cubes.

VEGETABLE TEMPURA WITH DIPPING SAUCE

½ medium sweet potato, cut into julienne strips
an equal quantity of butternut squash, cut into julienne strips
1 small red onion, cut in half and then thinly sliced
1 small red pepper, cut into slices
8 okra, cut into quarters lengthwise
oil for deep-frying
grated mooli (white radish) and grated ginger root to taste, to serve

For the dipping sauce
120ml/4fl oz shoyu or light soy sauce
120ml/4fl oz mirin
120ml/4fl oz water

For the batter
1 large free-range egg yolk
240ml/8fl oz iced water (place water in an icebox with a handful of ice; remove the ice before using)
150g/5oz tempura flour or sifted plain flour

Place the dipping sauce ingredients in a pan, bring to the boil and then gently simmer for a couple of minutes. Remove from the heat and pour into individual serving bowls.

To make the batter, mix the egg yolk with the iced water, taking care not to beat the mixture. Gently stir in the flour with chopsticks; it is normal for the batter to be lumpy (remember, handle the mixture as little as possible).

Dry the chopped vegetables in a tea towel or kitchen paper. Combine with the batter until well coated.

Deep-fry tablespoons of the mixture until golden and crispy. Remove from the pan and drain on kitchen paper before serving topped with grated mooli mixed with ginger and the dipping sauce on the side.

Mooli

Laos

LAZY DAYS ALONG THE MEKONG

Pages 116–117 **Buddha image at Wat Si Saket in Vientiane**

Below **View from Mount Phu Si**

Just before dawn every morning hundreds of young novice monks, dressed in saffron robes, walk barefoot in orderly lines through Luang Prabang. The purpose of their ambulation is to collect their daily meal in their alms bowls. The dimly lit city streets are lined with obliging townspeople, on their knees in reverence, eager to gain some morning merit and to play their part in this timeless ritual of Buddhist devotion.

Traditionally these mini monks can eat only what they receive during this morning ritual, so people give generously. The sight is truly spectacular and was well worth the early start, although as the morning progressed and hordes of other tourists joined the scene there began to be an element of watching a monk safari about it.

So we decided to take advantage of being up for the coolest part of the day and climb the town's monolithic Mount Phu Si. From the summit we could see stupas towering above the steaming monsoon forest in all directions and the mighty Mekong River snaking its way to the south on a journey we were about to make to the Cambodian border.

In Vientiane we dined on tofu *laap* with spicy papaya and sticky rice salads, and drank *beerlao* in an open-air café on the Mekong, as the sun set over Thailand across the river. We followed the river south to Pakse, capital of the Champasak province, Laos's third city and our entry port into the diverse landscape of southern Laos. First stop was the Bolaven plateau, an elevated jungle area of coffee plantations, bright green rice paddies, water buffalo wallowing in pits of muddy water, working elephants, waterfalls and tribal villages full of timeless tradition and smiling children.

One advantage of travelling here in the monsoon was spectacular waterfalls; the downside was the risk of heavy rain. We had been blessed with blue sky and sunshine for our treks to the Katu and Alak hill tribes, but our luck ran out in the Si Pham Don region. Meaning 'four thousand islands', this is the point where the Mekong is at its widest and splits into an inland delta to create thousands of islands of lush jungle between rapids. Despite the rain we had some amazing experiences travelling on a mixture of ferries, river boats and bicycles from Champasak to the Cambodian border. And at Wat Phu we saw Angkor-era Khmer temple ruins as atmospheric as any we would see in Cambodia.

FOOD IN LAOS

Eating in Laos is considered a social event; the saying 'Food eaten together tastes good, eaten alone tastes bad' is still important to most Laotians. In the cafés and food stalls, tables are always shared and the evening meal is seen as the perfect excuse to get together and party. When everyone is fuelled by *lau lau*, a rice whisky, they soon start singing the old ballads.

Laotians live off the land and whenever possible utilize seasonal wild foods, from mushrooms and ferns to game and honey. The markets perfectly reflect this: in the wet season when the rice paddies are full of croaking frogs, these become the most prolific ingredient on sale. Nothing is wasted: ants' eggs, lizards and insects are a common sight. They are sold side by side with packets of monosodium glutamate, which is used like salt. We learned to ask for dishes without seasoning, and without *pa dak,* the potent local fish sauce.

Luckily myriad seasonal vegetables are also available. In the wet season sweetcorn, mushrooms and bamboo shoots flourish. Green papayas, aubergines and long beans are plentiful. Local galangal root, lemon grass, chilli and garlic are pounded together using a pestle and mortar to flavour dishes, and then combined with sour flavours such as tamarind, lime juice and lime leaves.

Sticky or glutinous rice accompanies most meals: simply steamed, made into crunchy rice balls, toasted and ground, or even mixed with coconut milk and palm sugar to make a creamy sweet pudding.

Cooking generally still takes place on a clay brazier in the open, the fire imparting a wonderful smoky flavour. When all the dishes are cooked they are taken to the table and served at the same time. Fresh herbs and spicy zesty raw salads are an essential part of every meal.

The preparation of food plays a very important role in Buddhist festivals and ceremonies, and the early morning ritual of giving alms takes place daily throughout Laos.

Clockwise from top left **A green tea kettle; a street food market in Luang Prabang; a girl foraging for ferns on the Bolaven plateau; chillies, wood ear mushrooms and lemon grass at Pakse town market in Champasak; a variety of mushrooms on sale on a pavement in Pakse**

TOFU LARB

3 tablespoons sunflower oil
5 garlic cloves, sliced
4 spring onions, sliced
450g/1lb firm tofu, minced
6 tablespoons vegetable stock
1 tablespoon light soy sauce

The vegetables
225g/8oz fine green beans,
    thinly sliced
6 lime leaves, thinly sliced
2 spring onions, thinly sliced
5 shallots, thinly sliced
5 lemon grass stalks,
    thinly sliced

large handful of chopped
    coriander leaves

For the dressing
2 hot red chillies, sliced
3 tablespoons light soy sauce
juice of 2 large limes

To serve
large bunch of rocket
3 tablespoons sticky
    rice powder
large handful of mint leaves
½ cucumber, peeled and sliced

In a wok heat the oil. When hot, add the garlic and spring onion, and fry until golden. Add the tofu and continue to stir-fry until the tofu starts to brown.

Pour in the stock and soy sauce, and simmer until the stock has reduced. Turn out of the pan into a bowl and mix together the tofu, the vegetables and the combined dressing ingredients.

Line a large flat dish with rocket leaves and pile the tofu mixture on top. Sprinkle toasted rice powder over the mixture and garnish with mint leaves. Finally place the cucumber slices around the edge.

Larb is the quintessential Loa dish and is usually served with sticky rice rolled by hand into small balls that are dipped into a salad dressing. Crumbled tofu is fried with garlic and tossed with sliced lemon grass, toasted sticky rice powder, herbs and a spicy lime dressing.

Sliced banana flower is often an ingredient in *larb* but we find this quite hard to buy; green beans work just as well. If you have easy access to banana flowers, please substitute.

Ground toasted sticky rice powder is available ready made in Asian stores, but it is easily made by toasting raw sticky rice in a frying pan until golden, then grinding to a powder in a coffee grinder or using a pestle and mortar.

Tat Lo Lodge waterfall on the Bolaven plateau

Our driver's favourite, definitely worth stopping for!

AVOCADO SHAKE

SERVES 2 GREEDY PEOPLE
2 small soft ripe avocados
2 scoops vanilla ice cream
240ml/8fl oz chilled water
honey to taste
ice, to serve

Halve the avocados, remove the stone and scoop the flesh into a liquidizer. Add the remaining ingredients and blend until smooth. Pour into tall glasses over ice.

At Tat Lo on the Bolaven plateau we stayed in a simple log cabin. Built so close to a waterfall we could almost stretch out from the balcony and touch it, it became our home for the next few days. The resident cook went out of his way to provide us with vegetarian versions of local dishes. It was easy to spend hours just sitting on the balcony hypnotized by the waterfall. Occasionally a fisherman would appear below and wade into the rapids, throwing his weighted net into the water and then hauling it back with his catch. Lower down in a quieter pool, laughing children swam as women chatted over their washing.

On the road to the Bolaven plateau we stopped for lunch at a village our driver called 'barbecue village'. Its position next to a level crossing guaranteed it customers with a little time on their hands. Our driver chose his favourite café and ordered barbecued aubergine with spicy tomato dipping sauce and sticky rice.

The aubergine and peppers can be barbecued or griddled on the stove top. Blend any leftovers together to make a spicy dip.

This works really well with any barbecue dish but is equally tasty with sticky rice cakes.

If you are having a barbecue, cook the tomato, chilli peppers, shallots and garlic on the barbecue. Alternatively griddle on the stove top.

Bolaven barbecued red pepper and aubergine

BOLAVEN BARBECUED RED PEPPER AND AUBERGINE

2 medium aubergines, cut into lengthwise slices
2 red large red peppers, cut into thickish strips

For the dressing
3 tablespoons light soy sauce
juice of 2 limes
2 teaspoons honey

To garnish
4 spring onions, shredded
2 hot red chillies, cut into thin strips
handful of basil leaves
handful of coriander leaves

Brush the aubergine and pepper with oil and barbecue or griddle until soft. Cut the aubergine into strips (a similar width to the red peppers).

Whisk the soy sauce, lime juice and honey together to make a dressing. Carefully toss with the aubergine and peppers and pile on to a serving plate.

Garnish with spring onions, chillies and herbs and serve while still warm.

SPICY TOMATO DIPPING SAUCE

MAKES ABOUT 240ML/8FL OZ
250g/9oz cherry tomatoes
4 hot red chillies (or to taste)
6 garlic cloves
½ red pepper
2 shallots, halved
handful of coriander
2 tablespoons soy sauce

Barbecue or griddle the tomatoes, chilli, garlic, red pepper and shallots until soft.

Allow to cool a little and then blend with the soy sauce and coriander to make a roughly chopped sauce.

LUANG PRABANG BREAKFAST

SERVES 2

4 medium free-range eggs
knob of butter
1 scant tablespoon light
   soy sauce
good shake of black pepper
3 spring onions, finely sliced
½ teaspoon ground
   Sichuan pepper

1 sliced hot red chilli
   (optional), to garnish

To serve
baguette
condensed milk to taste

Beat the eggs with the soy sauce, black pepper and a pinch of salt.

Melt the butter in a frying pan. When hot, add the spring onions and Sichuan pepper, cook for a minute or so and then pour in the beaten eggs. Stir with a wooden spoon until the eggs are scrambled. Remove from the heat when just set and still soft.

Serve immediately, garnished with sliced chilli if you wish and with buttered warm baguette on the side. For the complete experience, drizzle condensed milk on warm baguette.

After our early morning expeditions into town, we returned to our hotel more than ready for breakfast. Baguette, originally introduced by the French, is now a Laotian breakfast staple. We ordered Laos-style scrambled egg, sweet Lao coffee and the local breakfast snack of warm baguette split in half and drizzled with condensed milk.

Left **Wat Phu Khmer Temple**

The morning markets start early in Laos and, determined not to miss out, we would drag ourselves out of bed while it was still dark outside. It all became worthwhile when we arrived at our favourite stall selling sweet coconut and honey pancakes.

Rice flour and sticky rice (glutinous rice) flour are available in Asian and good food stores.

TOASTED COCONUT AND HONEY PANCAKES

MAKES ABOUT 16
2 large free-range eggs
240ml/8fl oz coconut milk
1 tablespoon runny honey
80g/3oz rice flour
40g/1½ oz sticky rice flour
pinch of salt
½ teaspoon baking powder
oil for frying

To serve
handful of desiccated
    coconut dry roasted in a
    frying pan until golden
runny honey

Whisk the eggs with the coconut milk, honey and 60ml/2fl oz cold water.

Combine the rice flours, salt and baking powder in a bowl. Make a well in the middle and stir in the coconut milk mixture until a smooth batter forms. Leave to stand for 10 minutes.

In a small non-stick frying pan heat a little oil. When hot, pour in enough batter to coat the bottom of the pan. Cook until golden on both sides, turning when bubbles rise and the batter has set.

For each pancake, sprinkle with toasted coconut, drizzle with honey and roll. Eat immediately while still hot.

Right **Toasted coconut and honey pancakes**

FEU KHUA FRIED RICE NOODLES

450g/1lb flat rice noodles
sunflower oil for frying
3 large free-range eggs,
    beaten
1 medium red onion, sliced
2 hot red chillis, sliced
4 garlic cloves, crushed
250g/9oz oyster mushrooms,
    sliced
350g/12oz Asian greens, sliced
175g/6oz tinned shredded
    bamboo shoots, drained
    and rinsed in cold water
10 cherry tomatoes,
    cut into quarters

4 tablespoons vegetarian
    oyster sauce
1 tablespoon light soy sauce
1 teaspoon honey
2 teaspoons cornflour, mixed
    with a little water to make a
    thin paste
½ teaspoon ground
    white pepper

To garnish
handful of chopped coriander
large handful of bean sprouts
light soy sauce mixed with
    chopped chilli to taste

Cook the noodles as instructed on the packet, drain and
rinse well.

Heat 3 tablespoons of sunflower oil in a wok. When hot, add
the noodles and stir-fry for a few minutes. Stir in the beaten
egg and continue to stir-fry until the egg is cooked and the
noodles are well coated. Remove from the wok and set to
one side.

Heat a further 2 tablespoons of sunflower oil in the wok.
When hot, add the onion, chilli and garlic, and stir-fry until
soft. Add the mushrooms, greens, bamboo shoots and 120ml/
4fl oz water, and cook until the greens start to wilt.

Add the cherry tomatoes, oyster and soy sauces, honey,
cornflour paste and pepper. Simmer until the sauce thickens.

Return the noodles to the wok and stir-fry until well mixed
and piping hot. Serve immediately, garnished with chopped
coriander and bean shoots. Season with chilli soy sauce
to taste.

On the night of the full
moon festival at Wat
Phuang Kaew Temple,
we found an impromptu
food stall selling rice
noodles fried with egg,
oyster mushrooms and
Chinese spinach.

Feu khua can be made
with any Asian greens
such as choi sum or
Chinese broccoli. Chard,
spinach or even purple
sprouting broccoli make
good alternatives.

**Hill tribe villager
smoking opium**

As we arrived at the ferry point to cross the Mekong, the ferry was just leaving. Taking a positive attitude to the delay, we decided to cruise the food stalls in search of an impromptu lunch. We ordered steamed bamboo shoots, green beans, shitake and pak choi in a pounded peanut, galangal, lemon grass, tomato and coconut milk sauce.

Mekong peanut sauce is incredibly versatile. It is also used to season sweetcorn cobs, to dress rice noodles or simply as a dipping sauce.

Red curry paste can be bought from good food shops and Asian stores. Just check that the paste doesn't contain fish sauce.

You can use almost any vegetables but this is the combination we enjoyed in Laos.

MEKONG PEANUT SAUCE

MAKES ABOUT 480ML/16FL OZ

1 tablespoon sunflower oil
3 garlic cloves, crushed
3 shallots, finely diced
2cm/ ¾in piece of galangal, peeled and grated
½ teaspoon chilli flakes (optional)
1 teaspoon ground paprika
110g/4oz natural, unsalted, skinned peanuts, ground
  until finely chopped
1 tablespoon red curry paste
5 cherry tomatoes, diced
240ml/8fl oz coconut milk
1 teaspoon honey
2 tablespoons light soy sauce
2 lemon grass stalks, bashed with a rolling pin
2 lime leaves
2 tablespoons lime juice

In a wok heat the oil. When hot, add the garlic and shallots and stir-fry until soft.

Add the galangal, chilli flakes, paprika and ground peanuts. Stir-fry until the peanuts start to brown.

Stir in the red curry paste, followed by the tomatoes. Finally add all the remaining ingredients and gently simmer for about 10 minutes, until the sauce thickens, stirring occasionally to prevent sticking.

Remove the lemon grass and lime leaves before serving.

STEAMED VEGETABLES AND PEANUT SAUCE

FOR 2
75g/3oz tinned shredded bamboo shoots, drained and well rinsed
4 shitake mushrooms, quartered
150g/5oz fine green beans, top and tailed
2 small heads pak choi, stems sliced and leaves left whole
peanut sauce to taste

Steam the vegetables until al dente.

In a wok heat the peanut sauce, add the steamed vegetables and toss until well combined.

Clockwise from right Young monks collecting morning alms in Tat Lo village on the Bolaven plateau; Wat Si Saket in Vientiane; Pha That Luang stupa in Vientiane; monks in Luang Prabang town on their morning walk to collect alms

There were living Buddhist temples in every village in Si Pham Don, and late one night after dinner we went for a stroll along the Mekong, returning back to our guesthouse via the Wat Phuang Kaew Monastery with its huge seated golden Buddha. We noticed something stir and saw the magical sight of four young monks, lying asleep in the arms of the Buddha, bathed in the light of the full moon.

STICKY RICE

Measure the sticky rice in a measuring jug for the best results. 240ml/8fl oz of sticky rice is an average serving for four or generous for three, depending on appetite. The general rule is to add an equal quantity of water to the sticky rice when cooking, for every 240ml/8fl oz rice add 240ml/8fl oz cold water.

Wash the rice until the water runs clear. Place in a saucepan and add the correct measurement of cold water.

Bring the rice to the boil, cover the pan and reduce the heat. Gently simmer for 10 minutes. Turn off the heat and leave the lid on for a further 10 minutes.

Remove the lid and fluff the rice with a fork. Remember it is sticky rice – the grains should stick together.

Steamed sticky or glutinous rice is served in lidded woven baskets at the table; the rice is rolled into small balls by hand and then dipped into the different dishes on offer. When the meal is finished, it is considered bad luck not to replace the lid.

In Laos rice is soaked overnight and steamed, but at home we use this much easier method.

Any leftover rice can be stored in a plastic bag in the fridge and used for Crispy Rice Cakes.

At a riverside café on the banks of the mighty Mekong River we watched our supper of sticky rice cake salad being made. Sticky rice was mixed with coconut milk, grated coconut and curry paste, shaped into patties and fried until crunchy, and served with a simple watercress salad dressed with chilli, soy, lime, honey and spicy tomato sauce.

This recipe is a great way to use up leftover sticky rice. Red curry paste is available in good food shops and Asian stores – just make sure it is the vegetarian kind.

Children in a village on the Bolaven plateau

CRISPY RICE CAKES

MAKES ABOUT 18

60ml/2fl oz coconut cream or thick coconut milk
1 tablespoon red curry paste
25g/1oz desiccated coconut
1 teaspoon honey
splash of light soy sauce

450g/1lb cooked sticky rice (about a cup's worth of uncooked rice)
1 free-range egg, beaten
cornflour for dusting
oil for shallow-frying

Mix the coconut cream, red curry paste, desiccated coconut, honey and soy sauce together.

Combine with the cooked sticky rice and roll into balls (golfball size). Flatten each ball to make a pattie.

Coat the pattie with the beaten egg and dust with cornflour. Fry until golden brown and crunchy.

Serve with salad and spicy tomato sauce.

For the salad
Mix watercress with mint, cherry tomatoes, cucumber and sliced spring onions. Dress with equal amounts of soy sauce and lime juice and garnish with toasted ground natural peanuts.

Much of the urban architecture of Laos's newer capital, Vientiane, is a rather grim utilitarian legacy of the era of Soviet influence. A few gems of the past have survived intact, though, including what is probably one of the most beautiful monasteries in Laos, Wat Si Saket. Six and a half thousand Buddhas line the walls of the cloister surrounding the temple, many set into alcoves. We had the great privilege of being present when a priest induction ceremony was taking place, and as is the way with the Buddhist religion we were made to feel very welcome. We sat quietly at the back as prayers and vows were chanted, taking in the beauty of the frescoes lining the walls, depicting the story of Buddha. We couldn't be in Vientiane and not visit That Luang, the symbol of Laos, and it didn't disappoint: the huge golden multi-layered stupa looked surreal as it soared up into the blue sky.

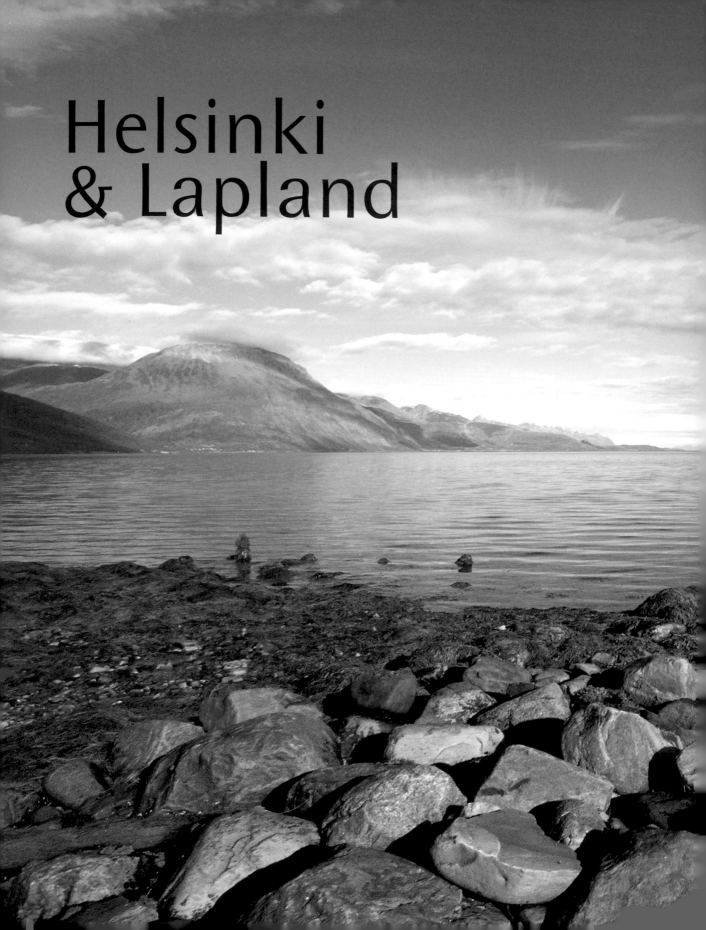

Helsinki
& Lapland

FROM THE BALTIC TO LAPLAND

Pages 134–135
**A Lapland landscape
in autumn**

Below **Reindeer being herded into their winter compound**

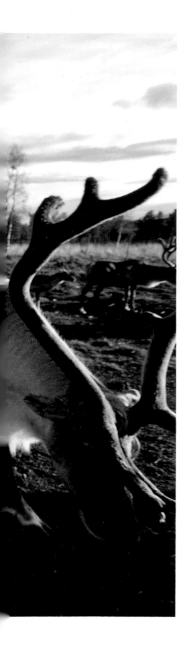

The Finnish capital Helsinki is one of Europe's best-kept secrets, simultaneously hip and historic, and a successful combination of urban elegance and natural beauty. It's a city where perfectly preserved Art Nouveau and classical Russian period buildings stand comfortably with cutting-edge contemporary architecture. The same country is home to semi-nomadic tribes of indigenous Sami reindeer herders, who still use tepees and consider themselves residents of Lapland, which if it were a country would include the northernmost regions of Finland, Sweden, Norway and Russia.

We timed our Lapland trip to be during the ruska season, when the landscape erupts into a spectacular explosion of autumn colours. It is a time of crystal-clear lakes, falling leaves, wild mushrooms, forest berries and reindeer migration, a narrow window between the summer mosquitoes and the sun disappearing for winter.

Although these days most Sami have the use of motor vehicles and permanent homes, the annual autumn reindeer migrations from highland summer pastures to lowland winter shelters still mean they must spend many nights in the wilderness sleeping in tepee-style *katas*. This is the best time of the year to visit a traditional Sami camp and share a stew of exquisite wild mushrooms cooked on an open fire, followed by baked cheese served with tangy, creamy cloudberries.

The seasons may not be quite so severe in Helsinki, but it's still a winter wonderland of glittering lights, frozen lakes and fresh snow for half of the year. In midsummer when temperatures soar and the sun hardly sets most of Helsinki's population migrate to their *mokkis* or summer cottages in the countryside. By August the city is buzzing again with open-air music festivals and street markets piled high with seasonal treats like sweet wild strawberries, peppery chanterelles and fresh herbs.

The market square on Helsinki harbour hums with the sounds of arrival and departure; the place is alive with smiling people, spending time with friends in cafés, riding bikes through parks, hopping on ferries to nearby islands, sunbathing on city beaches and tending to garden allotments. Helsinki is an easy-going city that seamlessly blends nature with modern urban life. It is also such a welcoming and user-friendly place that you effortlessly feel like a local within hours of being there.

FOOD IN HELSINKI & LAPLAND

The harsh Arctic climate has shaped the Finnish diet. In the dark snowy months there is a necessary reliance on root vegetables, dark rye breads and fermented dairy products; but then, for a few precious months, the sun shines and everything miraculously changes, and in the long sunny days, arctic berries, mushrooms, asparagus and wild herbs flourish.

Finnish cuisine is now a wonderful blend of traditional and contemporary cooking, combining high-quality Finnish produce with world influences. Cooking tends to be simple, with an emphasis on the freshest possible ingredients and healthy wholefood produce. The day starts with a hearty breakfast of muesli or porridge topped with berries, yoghurt, sour rye bread, boiled eggs and cheese.

In the summer when wild berries are prolific, foraged berries – a valuable source of nutrients – are liberally combined with savoury and sweet recipes; they are also preserved for the winter, dried, frozen or made into syrups, jams or juices.

Soon after midsummer, mushrooms raise their domed heads and the mushroom-hunting season starts in earnest. Mushrooms are enjoyed simply fried or made into flavoursome soups, sauces, bakes and stuffings, or dried and pickled for the winter.

Wholegrain rye, barley and oats are transformed into dense sour loaves, crispbreads and cereals. A traditional rye bread is made with a central hole, to facilitate hanging on wooden poles over the oven, where it gradually dries and can be stored for months.

Calcium-rich dairy produce such as yoghurt, sour cream, soft fresh quark cheese and mature Tilsit are favoured. The dense rubbery speciality 'squeaky' cheese is baked over the open fire and served with sweet berry compote. Creamy vegetable bakes, oven pancakes and rice pudding offer comfort in the dark winter months.

Coffee is practically the national drink; served strong, it is drunk by the gallon throughout the day. Finland has a long tradition of baking, so there is always a delicious spiced sweet bread or pastry to accompany a cup in one of the many friendly neighbourhood cafés.

Below, left to right
Berry stall in the market square in Helsinki; food in the design district; cooking in Sami Lavvu tepee in Lapland; cloud berries

BARLEYCRUST BAKED MUSHROOMS

1 medium onion, thinly sliced

3 tablespoons butter, plus some to dot on top of the bake

500g/1lb 2oz ceps or large flat mushrooms, sliced

1 tablespoon lemon juice

2 tablespoons plain flour

360ml/12fl oz double cream

2 large free-range eggs, beaten

1 tablespoon chopped thyme leaves

good grate of nutmeg

generous pinch of ground cloves

25g/1oz barley flakes or rolled jumbo oats

Preheat the oven to 200°C/400°F/gas mark 6.

Sauté the onions in butter until soft, taking care not to brown them. Add the sliced mushrooms and lemon juice, sauté for a further few minutes until the mushrooms start to soften and then stir in the flour. Turn out into a medium baking dish and set to one side.

Whisk the cream and the beaten eggs together. Add the thyme, nutmeg and ground cloves and season to taste with salt and ground white pepper.

Pour the cream mix over the mushrooms and place in the preheated oven. After 5 minutes or so, when the bake has started to set, carefully sprinkle barley flakes over the top and liberally dot with extra butter. Return to the oven and bake for a further 20 minutes, after which the bake should be golden and risen.

In autumn the forests are carpeted with wild mushrooms – chanterelles, ceps, milk caps, false morels and bright red russulas, to name but a few. It has been calculated that only 1 per cent of the annual mushroom growth is actually picked. The Laps are enthusiastic gatherers and a week-long festival celebrates their culinary importance. Freshly foraged mushrooms are baked with cream and eggs and a barley flake crust.

Ceps are delicious in this recipe but the humble large flat mushroom is equally good. Serve with a mixed leaf and herb salad or buttered steamed Savoy cabbage.

At breakfast our host made a simple dough mixture, shaped it into flat rounds and then baked them over the fire. We devoured the flatbreads while they were still warm, topped with butter and cheese and sweet but tart berry jam.

Flatbreads can be made from almost any wholemeal flour and are sometimes mixed with mashed potato or oats. In this recipe rye and barley flour are combined with buttermilk, which gives the slightly sour flavour that characterizes Finnish bread.

You can add other flavours to the bread such as raisins, sunflower or caraway seeds and top it with oats, barley flakes or linseed.

RYE AND BARLEY FLOUR FLATBREADS

MAKES 4 FLATBREADS

150g/5oz rye flour
175g/6oz barley or spelt flour
1½ teaspoons baking powder
½ teaspoon salt
2 tablespoons butter or olive oil

240ml/8fl oz buttermilk, yoghurt or whole milk

To top
rolled oats, barley flakes or linseed

Preheat the oven to 200°C/400°F/gas mark 6.

Combine the flours, baking powder and salt together. Rub in the butter, then add the buttermilk and mix together until a dough forms.

Divide the dough into quarters, dust with flour and shape into rounds 1cm/½in thick. Slightly moisten the top of the flatbreads with water. Sprinkle oats, rye flakes or linseed on top and gently press them into the dough.

Place on a greased baking tray and bake in the preheated oven for 15 minutes.

Rye and barley flour flatbreads

BEETROOT, JERUSALEM ARTICHOKE AND APPLE SALAD WITH A HORSERADISH SOUR CREAM DRESSING

5 medium Jerusalem artichokes,
   peeled and cubed
4 medium cooked beetroot,
   cubed
1 large tart apple, diced
2 carrots, cut into julienne strips
½ medium red onion,
   thinly sliced

For the dressing
2 tablespoons beetroot juice
juice of half a lemon

½ teaspoon honey
   or agave syrup
180ml/6fl oz sour cream
heaped teaspoon hot
   horseradish
small handful of chopped dill

To serve
mixed leaves such as sorrel,
   rocket, watercress, endive
   and frisée
handful of chopped walnuts

In the snow-filled months roots and tubers are a reliable vegetable source. Beetroot makes a colourful salad, especially when topped with a superb pink sour cream dressing. Use precooked beetroot (but make sure it doesn't contain vinegar) and retain the juice in the packet to add to the dressing.

Cook the Jerusalem artichokes in salted water until soft. Drain and rinse in cold water. Combine with the remaining ingredients.

Whisk the salad dressing ingredients together and season with salt and ground white pepper to taste.

Line a serving platter with the mixed leaves and pile the salad on top. Just before serving, drizzle with the sour cream dressing and garnish with chopped walnuts.

Left **Beetroot, Jerusalem artichoke and apple salad with a horseradish sour cream dressing**

Below **Pop-up food stall on Suomenlinna Island in Helsinki**

Finland is a land with an abundance of space and a tiny population. Sandwiched between Sweden and Russia, it stretches from the Baltic Sea to the Arctic Ocean. We travelled way up beyond the Arctic Circle to Europe's largest remaining forest wilderness, where we found some surprisingly good recipes using local ingredients. In the more sophisticated café culture of Helsinki, we ate delicious dishes created by inventive young chefs devoted to blending traditional Finnish ingredients with modern concepts of healthy eating.

CRANBERRY AND ORANGE SAUCE

350g/12oz fresh or frozen
   cranberries
zest of 1 medium orange
60ml/2fl oz orange juice
60ml/2fl oz unsweetened
   blueberry or black grape juice

1 vanilla pod, split
½ cinnamon stick
½ teaspoon ground ginger
honey or agave syrup to
   taste

Place all the ingredients in a saucepan and simmer until the cranberries are soft and break down to make a thick chunky sauce. Remove cinnamon stick before serving.

CREAMY SPLIT PEA AND MUSTARD SOUP

3 tablespoons butter
350g/12oz green split peas,
   soaked overnight, then
   drained and rinsed
1 large onion, diced
1 litre/1¾ pints vegetable
   stock
3 bay leaves

1 heaped tablespoon chopped
   marjoram leaves
1 heaped tablespoon chopped
   thyme leaves
3 carrots, diced
1 tablespoon hot mustard
1 tablespoon grainy mustard
90ml/3fl oz double cream

In a heavy-bottomed saucepan heat 2 tablespoons of butter, add the onion and sauté until soft. Stir in the drained split peas until coated with butter.

Pour in the stock, add the bay, marjoram and thyme, and simmer until the split peas start to soften. Add the diced carrot and continue to simmer until the carrots are soft.

Remove the bay leaves and lightly blend the soup until the peas break down but still retain some texture. Stir in the mustards, cream and remaining butter. Season to taste with salt and white pepper and simmer for a further few minutes to allow the flavours to combine.

In the summer months market stalls are piled high with arctic berries. The berries are lightly cooked to make thick fruity sauces, partnered with sweet and savoury dishes.

Cranberry and orange sauce can be served with savoury stuffed cabbage rolls and *rutmus* (see page 149), stirred into porridge or yoghurt, or simply spooned on to creamy rice pudding or pancakes.

In Lapland 'squeaky' cheese, a dense rubbery cheese made into flat rounds, is baked or grilled and topped with lingonberry or cranberry sauce. Halloumi cheese is the best substitute we have found. Slice the cheese, brush with a little oil and then griddle or fry until golden. Top with this cranberry sauce (lingonberries are almost impossible to find) and have some flatbread at hand to mop up the juices.

**A Sami Kata tepee
in the Finnish
countryside**

GLOGGI

2 cinnamon sticks
1 teaspoon cardamom seeds
heaped teaspoon cloves
5cm/2in piece of ginger root,
    peeled and sliced

1 bottle red wine
120ml/4fl oz vodka
1 large orange
brown sugar or honey to taste
blanched almonds and raisins,
    to serve

Place 120ml/4fl oz of water with the spices in a small saucepan with a fitted lid. Bring to the boil and gently simmer for 10 minutes. Strain the spice liquid into a medium saucepan and pour in the wine and vodka.

Peel the orange rind with a vegetable peeler and cut the orange into thick slices. Add both to the wine with sugar to taste. Gently simmer until aromatic.

Drop a few blanched almonds and raisins into the bottom of each glass before serving.

After our husky safari a steaming cauldron of spiced gloggi welcomed us home. To make gloggi, red wine is mulled with vodka and spices and then served in glasses with a few almonds and raisins dropped in the bottom.

A non-alcoholic gloggi is also made with blackcurrant juice. Follow the same method, substituting berry juice for the wine and omitting the vodka.

The husky dogs of Lapland, which work flat out all winter pulling sleighs, had little to do during the rest of the year, until someone came up with the brilliant idea of husky safaris. These involve putting on a harness and then being taken for a walk by a dog. Your husky follows a scented trail and leads you deep into the forest. Within minutes of leaving the starting point you have no sense of direction and feel blissfully alone with nature. It was an extraordinary experience to be totally dependent on an animal to find your way back home. Most huskies spend their lives entirely outdoors, however far below zero the mercury plummets; when not working they are chained to their kennels. But a chosen few are treated more like pets and allowed into the tepees at night to curl up next to a sleeping Sami. The night we spent in a tepee was so cold we were very grateful to be lent a couple of these breathing hot-water bottles.

Here the Finnish national dish is given a contemporary twist: Savoy cabbage leaves are stuffed with mushrooms and barley and flavoured with the summer herb sorrel. Serve with buttery mashed potato and cranberry sauce (see page 144).

You can use almost any mushroom in this dish. We tend to use chanterelles or ceps for a special occasion and brown caps for everyday.

Our husky, Peanut, in Lapland

SAVOY CABBAGE LEAVES STUFFED WITH MUSHROOMS AND BARLEY

MAKES 15

15 Savoy cabbage leaves
50g/2oz barley groats (or brown rice)
75g/3oz mushrooms, roughly chopped
1 small onion, diced
2 Savoy cabbage leaves, finely chopped
1 tablespoon chopped marjoram leaves

handful of sorrel leaves, sliced (or spinach with a squeeze of lemon)
60ml/2fl oz double cream
60ml/2fl oz quark
1 dessertspoon honey
120ml/4fl oz retained cabbage water
butter

Preheat the oven to 200°C/400°F/gas mark 6.

Cook the cabbage leaves in salted water until soft, drain (retaining the liquid) and cut away the thick lower stem of each leaf.

Cook the barley in salted water until soft, drain and combine in a food processor with the mushroom, onion, cabbage, marjoram and sorrel until finely chopped. Stir in the cream, quark and seasoning to taste.

Transform the cabbage leaves into parcels: place 2 tablespoons of the stuffing on each leaf, fold the sides in and tightly roll.

Sandwich the rolls side by side in a buttered baking dish. Add the cabbage water, drizzle with honey and liberally dot with butter.

Bake in the preheated oven for 30 minutes. Serve with buttery mashed potato, drizzled with cooking juices, and cranberry sauce on the side.

OVEN PANCAKES WITH STRAWBERRY AND BLUEBERRY COMPOTE

2 large free-range eggs
480ml/16fl oz whole milk
50g/2oz caster sugar
60g/2½oz plain flour
2 tablespoons melted butter
1 vanilla pod, split

For the compote
200g/7oz strawberries, quartered
110g/4oz blueberries
honey to taste

Preheat the oven to 200°C/400°F/gas mark 6.

Whisk the eggs until frothy; then beat in the milk and sugar. Gradually stir in the flour, followed by the melted butter.

Pour the batter into a generously greased 20cm/8in flan dish and place the vanilla pod in the centre. Bake in the preheated oven for 30 minutes or so, after which the pancake should be set, bubbling and golden brown. Allow the pancake to cool a little before attempting to cut it into slices.

To make the compote, lightly cook the berries in a pan with a splash of water and honey to taste.

Top the pancake slices with compote and a spoonful of crème fraîche.

Oven pancakes might traditionally be served for dessert on Thursdays, but why limit the pleasure? Serve for an indulgent Sunday brunch or an afternoon treat with a cup of strong coffee.

This thick pancake resembles baked custard and once cooled a little sets just enough to be cut into slices and served warm, topped with a berry compote and crème fraîche.

We found a great emphasis on healthy eating in Finnish cooking and foraging is an important part of Finnish culture. Healthy living is popular too: a passion for pinewood-smoke saunas is ubiquitous. Saunas, often located in wooden huts deep in a forest next to the sea or lakeshore, are more than just a leisure activity: they are seen as a source of natural pride and a celebration of a mystic past. The sauna ritual often includes feasting on seasonal produce and the rather less healthy practice of consuming copious amounts of vodka and schnapps. They may also feature a certain amount of blood-circulation-boosting self-flagellation with birch leaves and always end with a powerfully invigorating plunge into icy water. Even in the depths of the long dark freezing winter they are a way of relaxing and warming up with friends and family or even business associates. In the summer months a muscle-relaxing sauna is the perfect end to a long day's hiking or cycling through the pristine Finnish countryside.

In the summer months food stalls in Helsinki harbour's open-air market serve a good-value lunch menu, including classic Finnish dishes such as fluffy, smooth, creamy root vegetable *rutmus*, topped with cinnamon fried onions and grilled asparagus.

CREAMY PARSNIP, SWEDE AND POTATO RUTMUS

500g/1lb 2oz potatoes,
   peeled and diced
250g/9oz swede, diced
2 parsnips, diced
50g/2oz butter, diced
120ml/4fl oz double cream
asparagus, grilled or lightly
   cooked in boiling water,
   to serve (optional)

For the topping
1 large red onion, sliced
1 tablespoon olive oil
1 tablespoon butter
1 teaspoon ground cinnamon

Simmer the diced potato, swede and parsnip in salted water until soft. Drain and roughly mash until broken down. Whip with a hand whisk until really smooth. Add the butter and cream and whip again until fluffy. Season to taste with salt and ground white pepper.

To make the topping, sauté the sliced red onion in olive oil and butter until soft, add the ground cinnamon and continue cooking until the onions caramelize. Spoon on top of the *rutmus* before serving.

Autumn in Norwegian Lapland

Blackcurrant and blackberry sauce is partnered with red cabbage simmered with apple and spices – a sweet and sour taste combination popular in Finland.

Spiced red cabbage improves with age and works really well served cold the next day with cheese and thin slices of buttered rye bread.

If berries are out of season, look in the freezer section, as there are usually several options; you could even use a bag of frozen mixed berries.

Clockwise from top left **Church in Karesuando in northern Norway; landscape in northern Norway; elk in Lapland; cycling on Suomenlinna Island in Helsinki**

SPICED SIMMERED RED CABBAGE WITH BLACKCURRANT AND BLACKBERRY SAUCE

2 tablespoons butter
1 medium red onion, thinly sliced
500g/1lb 2oz thinly sliced red cabbage
2 medium tart apples, sliced
1 tablespoon honey
10 cloves
10 allspice
1 dessertspoon red wine vinegar

180ml/6fl oz unsweetened berry juice, such as blueberry or blackcurrant (red grape juice would also work)

For the berry sauce
knob of butter
150g/5oz blackcurrants (or blueberries)
150g/5oz blackberries
splash of berry juice (as above)
honey to taste

Melt the butter in a heavy-bottomed saucepan, add the onions, red cabbage, apple and honey, and sauté until the vegetables start to wilt. Add the remaining spices, vinegar and juice. Season with salt and ground white pepper to taste and gently simmer for about 30 minutes, until the liquid has reduced and the cabbage is nice and soft (add an extra splash of juice if necessary).

To make the sauce, melt a knob of butter in a small saucepan, add the berries and stir until coated with butter. Add a little juice and honey to taste. Simmer until the berries are soft and start to break down.

Serve the spiced cabbage with a spoonful of berry sauce and *rutmus* (see page 149).

Namibia

THE LONG ROAD TO NOWHERE

Pages 152–153
**A petrified forest in
the Sossusvlei Desert**

Below **Kaokoland landscape in northern Namibia**

As soon as you arrive at Windhoek airport in Namibia you feel as though you have left the rest of the world behind and entered a land where time has little meaning and humans are of little importance. This is a land of vast empty landscapes that stretch, boundless and bare, from horizon to horizon under immense skies. We found Namibia's emptiness refreshing, awesome and strangely seductive.

Just a short drive from the airport, Goche Ghanas is a desert habitat of benign African wildlife including white rhino, giraffe, zebra, wildebeest and a dozen other breeds of antelope. Because of the absence of any dangerous beasts, all these can be seen on casual unaccompanied walks in the bush. It was a good place to spend a few days before our very long drive to the sand sea of Sossusvlei. The only settlement of any size on the whole journey was appropriately called Solitaire, a very lonely outpost consisting of little more than a petrol station and a German bakery, where we picked up snacks for the rest of the journey. When we finally arrived we stayed at a place called Le Mirage Lodge, which looked like a French Foreign Legion fort, standing alone in the desert. From here we explored the surreal landscapes of giant sand dunes and petrified forests on dawn walks and moonlit quad-bike safaris. It was like being in a Salvador Dalí painting. Temperatures of 55°C/131°F made it even more extraordinary; it was the hottest place we have ever been.

The flight from here to Kaokoland was also stunning. Gliding over the elevated plateau of Damarland was like flying over the surface of another planet. Then we hit the shipwreck-strewn Skeleton Coast and followed it all the way to the Kunene River in Hartmann's Valley on the border with Angola. Here we met Himba people, members of one of the last nomadic tribes of Africa.

Finding vegetarian food in sub-Saharan Africa is always a challenge and even more so in desert areas, where no vegetables grow. Once we moved on to the fertile Caprivi Strip eating well became much easier: using local ingredients and a bit of imagination, we managed to find plenty of quick and easy recipes for things like spicy peanut and chickpea soup, *chakalaka* (a bean and pepper stew), and quince and butternut *potje*.

FOOD IN NAMIBIA

The flavours of Namibia are a unique melting pot of cuisines, characterized by tribal indigenous staples mixed with influences from Namibia's German colonial past and from South Africa, its nearest neighbour. Apple strudel and black forest gateau are as popular as cornmeal porridge with *chakalaka* stew.

Historically hunter gathering provided the essential ingredients of survival; wild fruits, nuts, beans, leaves and game are still prominent in Namibian cooking. Cattle are considered the most treasured possession in the Herero tribe, with milk, butter, yoghurt and cheese forming the bulk of their diet, whereas thick cornmeal porridge served with spicy gravy is the staple diet of the Himba tribe.

Potje stews are cooked over an open fire in characteristic cast-iron three-legged pots and shared communally: potato, celery, squash, kale, peppers and tomatoes are slowly simmered with cloves, cinnamon, allspice, ginger and nutmeg.

The *braai* or barbecue becomes a pot-luck party at sunset; the rule is that everyone brings a dish and something to barbecue. With a plentiful supply of sundowners on tap, the party lasts well into the warm night.

Dried fruits add sweetness to marinades and chutneys, peanuts and beans provide protein; and with the addition of herbs and aromatic spices simple recipes are transformed.

The German tradition of baking makes an indulgent addition to Namibian cuisine; cakes, pies, pasties and bakes are still popular. As is the locally brewed German-style lager, practically the national drink and a perfect antidote to a dusty journey. Alternatively rooibus herbal tea is a tasty indigenous pick-me-up, thought to be full of health-giving properties.

With Namibia having one of the lowest populations in Africa, restaurants are few and far between. We looked forward to our pit stops after hours of driving through the wild and wondrous landscapes of Namibia.

A camp belonging to the nomadic Himba people of Kaokoland

APRICOT BLATJANG

MAKES ABOUT TWO 450G/1LB JARS

200g/7oz dried apricots, roughly chopped	small red onion, diced
480ml/16fl oz boiling water	handful of raisins
2cm/¾in piece of ginger root, peeled and grated	1 cinnamon stick
1 garlic clove, crushed	¼ teaspoon ground cloves
1 red chilli, finely chopped	grated zest of half an orange
	1 tablespoon brown sugar
	30ml/1fl oz cider vinegar

Place the chopped apricots in a bowl and cover with the boiling water. Leave to stand for half an hour.

Blend the ginger, garlic, chilli and onion in a food processor until finely chopped. Drain the apricots (retaining the water), add to the processor and blend once more until the soaked apricots are roughly chopped.

Pour the retained apricot water into a saucepan and stir in the apricot and onion mix. Add the raisins, cinnamon, ground cloves, orange zest, sugar and vinegar. Gently simmer until the water has reduced and the chutney has a thick jam-like consistency.

The chutney is ready to use immediately or can be stored in a sterilized jars in the fridge.

BARBECUE BRAII MARINADE

Mix a splash of freshly squeezed orange juice, olive oil, soy and chilli sauce with chopped red chilli and garlic to make a sweet but savoury marinade for halloumi cheese, sweetcorn cobs, pumpkin and sweet potato. The sugar caramelizes beautifully on the barbecue.

Blatjang, made from dried fruit and spices, is a cross between a chutney and a jam. It adds sweetness to *potje* stews and barbecue marinades or accompanies savoury bakes.

Spicy black-eyed peas

Simple but tasty, black-eyed peas simmered in a spicy stock are traditionally served with *oshifima*, a cornmeal porridge. We prefer to serve them with wilted spinach or lightly cooked fine green beans and apricot *blatjang*. The peas should be quite hot, but adjust the seasoning to taste.

SPICY BLACK-EYED PEAS

350g/12oz black-eyed peas, soaked in water overnight
1–2 teaspoons dried chilli flakes (to taste)
a few sprigs of thyme
4 celery sticks, diced
small handful of chopped chives

Drain and rinse the black-eyed peas, place in a saucepan and cover with water. Add the chilli flakes and thyme, cover the pan and gently simmer until nearly soft; then add the celery and seasoning to taste. Continue to simmer until the black-eyed peas are soft.

Sprinkle with chopped chives and a little extra chilli flakes.

PEPPERS BAKED WITH POMEGRANATE AND GREEN PEPPERCORNS

SERVES 4

4 medium red peppers, cut in half and seeds removed
120ml/4fl oz pomegranate seeds
2 tablespoons green peppercorns
handful of roughly chopped raisins
handful of green olives, sliced
4 garlic cloves, finely chopped

1 dessertspoon chopped fresh thyme
olive oil

To serve
Sweet potato mashed with lots of butter and seasoned with ground cinnamon and black pepper to taste

Preheat the oven to 190°C/375°F/gas mark 5.

Place the red pepper halves in a baking tray.

Combine the pomegranate seeds, peppercorns, raisins, olives, garlic and thyme.

Spoon the mixture into the prepared red pepper halves, drizzle liberally with olive oil and season to taste. Bake in the preheated oven for 45 minutes.

Serve with cinnamon-spiced mashed sweet potatoes.

Baked red peppers stuffed with pomegranate seeds, raisins, green peppercorns and chopped green olives, and served on a bed of buttery mashed sweet potatoes.

Green peppercorns are sold preserved in brine in jars; alternatively soak dried green peppercorns in boiling water for 15 minutes before use.

Chakalaka, a spicy bean, pepper and tomato stew, is often made with tinned baked beans for the ultimate shortcut. Using tinned haricot beans with chopped tomatoes and a little honey is almost as quick and much tastier. Top with grated mature Cheddar cheese.

CHAKALAKA

4 tablespoons olive oil
1 large onion, diced
4 garlic cloves, crushed
4cm/1½in piece of ginger root, peeled and grated
3 hot red chillies, sliced
1 small red pepper, diced
1 small green pepper, diced
2 grated carrots
3 celery sticks, diced
2 teaspoons good curry powder
1 scant teaspoon ground allspice
3 bay leaves
1½ tins (400g/14oz size) haricot beans, drained and rinsed
400g/14oz tin chopped plum tomatoes
300ml/10fl oz vegetable stock
2 tablespoon tomato purée
1 tablespoon peri peri or Tabasco sauce
1 dessertspoon honey
grated mature Cheddar cheese, to serve (optional)

Heat the oil in a heavy-bottomed saucepan. When hot, add the onion, garlic, ginger and chilli. Cook until the onion starts to soften and then add the diced pepper, carrot and celery. Sauté until the vegetables are soft.

Add the curry powder, allspice and bay leaves. Then stir in the beans, chopped plum tomatoes, vegetable stock, tomato purée, peri peri and honey.

Gently simmer until the sauce has reduced and the oil returns. Season to taste with salt and freshly ground black pepper. If you like, serve with grated cheese.

Elephants drinking on a river bank in the Caprivi Strip

Driving long distances was never too arduous in Namibia, as there was never any other traffic to worry about and the roads were in mint condition. Although the landscape changed slowly, there were often visual treats like a long line of zebra walking across the desert miles from anywhere or a lone oryx silhouetted against a rising moon. When the moon was full it was bright enough to read a book, so cooking in roadside camps was easy even at night.

Hippos in the Caprivi Strip, oryx and an elephant in Etosha, and a kingfisher on the Zambezi

ICED ROOIBUS TEA SUNDOWNERS

6 rooibus teabags
3cm/1¼ in piece of ginger
    root, peeled and grated
1 large orange, cut into slices
1 lemon, cut into slices
3 cloves

1 cinnamon stick
1 tablespoon honey

To serve
fresh squeezed orange juice
    and gin to taste
ice

Place all the ingredients in a saucepan with 1.2 litres/2 pints water and bring to the boil. Reduce the heat and gently simmer for 5 minutes. Leave to cool and strain into a jug.

Serve over ice with a little freshly squeezed orange juice and an optional slug of gin.

As the sun set and the full moon rose, we drank a toast to the Namibian desert.

Rooibus tea from the native red bush tree brewed with cinnamon, ginger and orange makes a refreshing iced tea. Mixed with gin, it sets the evening off with a swing.

The strange shape of the Caprivi Strip, a narrow appendage squeezed in between Angola and Botswana, is a legacy of the colonial squabbles in Africa. Claimed by the British in the nineteenth century as the Bechuanaland Protectorate, it was traded with the Germans in 1890, along with Heligoland Island in the North Sea, in exchange for Zanzibar. It was renamed Caprivi after a German count and made part of German South West Africa, much to the disapproval of the Lozi people who lived there and left in protest. On 4 August 1914, the day that the First World War was declared in Europe, the German governor of Caprivi was entertaining the British resident of nearby Northern Rhodesia (now Zambia) when a telegram arrived from Livingstone informing his dinner guest of the news. Once the meal was over the Englishman thanked his host, then drew his pistol and informed him that he was under arrest as a prisoner of war, and that a battalion of British troops was on its way to claim the strip as the first Allied territorial gain of the war.

In the one-horse outpost of Solitaire, the local provisions store doubles as a café, where the dish of the day when we arrived was spicy peanut and chickpea soup, served with chunks of buttered rye bread.

SPICY PEANUT AND CHICKPEA SOUP

3 tablespoons olive oil
1 large onion, diced
2 garlic cloves, crushed
thumb-sized piece of ginger
    root, peeled and grated
2 hot red chillies,
    finely chopped
1 teaspoon ground cinnamon
½ teaspoon cracked
    black pepper
1 medium potato,
    peeled and cubed

400g/14oz peeled, deseeded
    pumpkin, cut into chunks
1 large green pepper, diced
175g/6oz kale, thinly sliced
1.2 litres/2 pints vegetable
    stock
400g/14oz tin of chickpeas,
    drained and rinsed
60ml/2fl oz smooth peanut
    butter

Heat the olive oil in a heavy-bottomed saucepan. When hot, add the onion, garlic, ginger and chilli, sauté until soft and then stir in the cinnamon and pepper.

Add the potato, pumpkin and pepper, and cook until the vegetables start to soften.

Add the kale, stock and chickpeas, cover the pan and gently simmer until the vegetables are soft.

Dissolve the peanut butter in a little boiling water and then stir it into the soup. Season to taste and gently simmer for a further couple of minutes. Serve with buttered rye bread.

The lone café/shop in Solitaire

CREAMY POTATO AND MUSHROOM BAKE

3 medium potatoes, peeled
  and thinly sliced
1 medium onion, thinly sliced
2 garlic cloves, finely chopped
1 dessertspoon chopped
  fresh thyme
freshly grated nutmeg,
  to taste

1 large sweet potato, peeled
  and sliced slightly thicker
  than the potatoes
225g/8oz large flat
  mushrooms, sliced
200ml/7fl oz double cream
120ml/4fl oz vegetable stock
butter, to dot on the bake

Preheat the oven to 190°C/375°F/gas mark 5.

Line a baking dish with the potato slices, add a third of the onion, garlic and thyme, and season with black pepper, a little salt and a generous serving of freshly grated nutmeg. Continue to layer with the sweet potato and mushroom slices, using the same method. Finally cover the bake with any potato and sweet potato slices left.

Pour the cream and stock evenly over the top and dot with butter.

Cover with kitchen foil and bake in the preheated oven for 45 minutes. Then remove the foil, increase the oven temperature to 200°C/400°F/gas mark 6 and bake for a further 15–20 minutes, until golden.

As the sun set we lit the *braai* for a classic Namibian barbecue. Any *braai* is incomplete without a potato bake, in which slices of potato, sweet potato and mushroom are layered with onion and then baked in cream and nutmeg.

Creamy potato and mushroom bake

QUINCE AND BUTTERNUT SQUASH POTJE

2 tablespoons olive oil
1 tablespoon butter
1 large onion, sliced
3 garlic cloves, finely chopped
thumb-sized piece of ginger
  root, peeled and finely
  chopped
½ teaspoon ground cloves
½ teaspoon ground nutmeg
2 medium quinces, peeled,
  cored and sliced
2 carrots, sliced on a diagonal
3 celery sticks, sliced

3 medium potatoes,
  peeled and sliced
peeled, deseeded and sliced
  butternut squash
  (roughly the same quantity
  as the potato)
1 teaspoon ground ginger
1 teaspoon ground turmeric
1 teaspoon ground paprika
½ teaspoon ground
  black pepper
1 cinnamon stick
3 tablespoons apricot chutney
420ml/14fl oz vegetable stock

Heat the olive oil and the butter in a heavy-bottomed pan. When hot, add the onion, garlic and ginger, sauté until soft and then stir in the ground cloves and nutmeg.

Remove the pan from the heat and layer the fruit and vegetables on top of the fried onion, starting with quince slices and finishing with butternut squash.

Sprinkle in the remaining spices and dot with the chutney. Season the vegetable stock and pour over the *potje*. Cover the pan, return it to the heat and gently simmer until the vegetables are soft and the stock has reduced.

Our guide layered quince and squash over spiced onions in a cast-iron three-legged *potje*. As it slowly cooked, we sat around the fire and put the world to rights with the help of a cold beer or two.

A *potje* was too difficult to pack in our luggage, so we now use a cast-iron saucepan with a fitted lid to make this recipe.

Quince is a hard pear-shaped fruit with a slight bloom on the skin and a perfumed flavour. It discolours when cut, so once you have prepared it, place it in a bowl of water with a good squeeze of lemon, until you are ready to use it.

If you find quince difficult to buy, pears or apples make a good substitute. In Namibia apricot chutney is a popular addition to recipes, but mango chutney also works well.

A spiced yeast-free bread, concocted by German settlers as an easy method of making bread when far away from home.

SPICED VELDT BREAD

450g/1lb wholemeal flour
4 teaspoons baking powder
1 teaspoon ground cinnamon
½ teaspoon ground allspice
¼ teaspoon ground cloves
pinch of salt

50g/2oz brown sugar
75g/3oz unsalted butter, diced
1 large free-range egg
150ml/5fl oz whole milk

Preheat the oven to 200°C/400°F/gas mark 6.

Sift the flour, baking powder, cinnamon, allspice, clove and salt into a large bowl. Add the sugar and rub in the butter. Make a well in the centre.

Whisk the egg and milk together, pour into the well and combine until a thick dough forms. Dust with a little extra flour and knead the dough until it becomes nice and elastic (knead for as long as you can bear: you will be rewarded with a good textured bread).

Turn out into a greased and then floured bread tin or shape into a round. Score the top and place on a greased baking sheet.

Bake in the preheated oven for 45 minutes. The bread should sound hollow when tapped on the bottom.

A solitary tree among dunes in the Sossusvlei Desert

Syria

ROAD TRIP THROUGH HISTORY

Pages 170–171 **The magnificent historic site of Palmyra**

Damascus is the oldest continually inhabited city in the world. We visited it in the spring of 2010, in what we did not realize were to be some of the last days of peace, and we found that exploring the labyrinths of the old city was like stepping back into a more romantic past. In ornate courtyard cafés families and friends gathered to eat meze plates of local delicacies, drink mint tea or wine, smoke hubble-bubble pipes of scented tobacco and listen to storytellers. In the covered souks merchants sold everything from silk and spices to folk medicines and perfumes. Down winding alleys wafts of scented steam escaping from hammams mixed with the aromas of freshly cooked snacks from street stalls. The freshest possible locally grown produce soon had our stomachs rumbling and full of anticipation for meals that lay ahead.

Finding good food in Damascus required little effort and it was an easy place to be vegetarian, with so many meze dishes made of vegetables, fruits, pulses, herbs and grains and so many places to eat, from street stalls to grand open-air rooftop restaurants.

After a few days we hired a car and headed up country. First stop was the ancient Christian settlement of Ma'loula in the Qalamoun Mountains, where people still use the biblical language of Aramaic. At Krak des Chevaliers, described by Lawrence of Arabia as 'the best preserved and most wholly admirable castle in the world', we had a fine lunch of baby aubergines with barberries, apricots and pine nuts. On the Mediterranean coast we spent a day among the ruins of the Phoenician city of Amrit, built in the fifteenth century BC. Its lofty funerary towers have carved lions around their base and there is a rock-cut sports stadium that predates Olympia.

Our longest drive was from here inland to the remains of the Roman city of Palmyra in the eastern desert. As one of the best-preserved sites of classical antiquity anywhere in the world, this was Syria's premier tourist site. Inevitably this had compromised the quality of the food on offer, save the always reliable Syrian breakfast of warm bread, honey, yoghurt, olives and *lebneh* (a soft cheese) and lots of steaming cardamom coffee.

Souk Al-Bezuriye in the old city of Damascus

FOOD IN SYRIA

The labyrinth of streets that make up Damascus's famous souk were lined with stalls piled high with olives, figs, dates, pomegranates, pulses, herbs and spices. Beautifully displayed and locally grown deep purple aubergines, bulbous peppers, cucumbers and the ripest tomatoes tempted shoppers looking for inspiration for the day's cooking.

Mealtimes were a boisterous family affair, starting meze style. The table was decorated with a wide selection of appetizing small dishes, ranging from delicious dips and olives to stuffed vine leaves. Colourful salads followed, such as finely chopped parsley mixed with cracked wheat and tomato or fattoush, a salad dressed with lemon and sumac. Accompanying every meal were generous servings of flatbread, which was torn and used in the place of utensils to scoop up dainty mouthfuls. Kebabs and kibbeh finished the meal. In the evening dessert was preferably eaten out in cafés, providing a chance to take a stroll, catch up and socialize. Elaborately decorated gateaux competed for attention with tooth-numbingly sweet baklava, the perfect accompaniment to thick black Turkish coffee and a hookah.

Black tea was drunk throughout the day and street stalls selling *ful* (broad beans) cooked with cumin, garlic and lemon, or hot falafel wrapped in flatbread, were always available.

Bread is revered as the staff of life; to waste it is considered a shame. As a sign of respect, it is always torn and never cut with a knife. Sheep's milk yoghurt is made into a simple fresh soft cheese flavoured with herbs and olive oil or blended with mint to make a cooling yoghurt drink. The essential Syrian ingredient tahini, made from ground sesame seeds, is mixed with pulses or baked aubergine to create smoky meze dips or simply mixed with lemon juice and garlic to make indispensable tahina sauce.

Courtyard café in the old city of Damascus

Courtyard of the
Umayyad Mosque

At the Umayyad Mosque or Great Mosque of Damascus we spent
many hours just relaxing into the happy atmosphere and watching
the world go by. Far more than just a place of worship, this is the
heart of the old city. Children played and slid about on the polished
marble floor of the vast open courtyard between black-veiled Iranian
pilgrims, bejewelled Gulf Arabs and Egyptian tourists. Around the
edge groups of friends relaxed and chatted in the shade, had picnics,
napped or even played games on their mobile phones; everyone
was welcome. In the vast prayer hall there was a shrine to John the
Baptist and just outside a modest mausoleum containing the remains
of Saladin.

AYRAN YOGHURT DRINK

480ml/16fl oz full-fat
   natural yoghurt
360ml/12fl oz cold still
   mineral water

salt to taste
handful of fine chopped
   mint leaves
ice to serve

Whisk the yoghurt and water together until frothy. Stir in salt
to taste.
   Quarter fill a tall glass with ice, pour over the yoghurt mix
and sprinkle with finely chopped fresh mint.

A cooling mint
and yoghurt drink,
traditionally served
by the Bedouin. Salt is
added to the yoghurt to
replace salt lost from the
body during long hot
desert journeys.

Crisp toasted pitta bread, fresh herbs, vegetables and crumbled feta cheese, drizzled with a lemon juice and sumac dressing, made a superb lunch on the road to the dramatic Crusaders' castle Krak des Chevaliers.

FATTOUSH SALAD

For the salad
2 pitta breads
½ medium Cos or 1 Romaine lettuce, thinly sliced
1 green pepper, diced
3 medium tomatoes, diced
2 small cucumbers, peeled and diced
8 radish, cubed
4 spring onions, sliced
large handful of finely chopped parsley

handful of roughly chopped mint
1 tablespoon sumac (see Za'atar, page 183) or 1 teaspoon ground paprika
crumbled feta cheese (optional), to serve

For the dressing
1 garlic clove, crushed
4 tablespoons lemon juice
6 tablespoons, olive oil
salt and pepper to taste

Toast the pitta bread until crisp, tear into bite-size pieces and set to one side.

Gradually combine the salad vegetables and herbs with the sumac. Whisk the dressing ingredients together.

Just before serving, pour the dressing over the salad. Add the toasted pitta and toss together. Serve immediately, topped with crumbled feta cheese if desired.

Built by Crusaders on their way to do battle with Saladin, the castle of Krak des Chevaliers still stands in all its glory on a hill-top above the village of Al-Husn. The castle was so strong that it was never captured by force in its military history and legend has it that it held enough supplies to feed two thousand men for five years.

SYRIAN BREAKFAST

Syrian breakfast, served meze style, was definitely worth getting up for. Back home, Sunday mornings are never now complete without recreating the unforgettable flavours of Syria.

Partner *labneh*, topped with fresh herbs and fruity olive oil, with thick slices of cucumber and tomato, olives and warm flatbread. Finish with a bowl of sheep's milk yoghurt with runny honey drizzled over it, and cardamom coffee to drink.

LABNEH

240ml/8fl oz sheep's milk
  yoghurt
1 teaspoon cumin seeds
½ teaspoon salt
handful of chopped mint
  leaves
small handful of chopped
  dill leaves

olive oil
black pepper

To serve
tomato and baby cucumber
  slices
olives
warm unleavened bread
yoghurt and honey

Labneh is very easy to make. Leave overnight to strain and it will be ready to eat in the morning.

Line a plastic sieve with muslin and place over a bowl deep enough for the drained whey not to touch the sieve.

Mix the yoghurt with the cumin seeds and salt, and scoop into the muslin-lined sieve. Leave in a cool place overnight. The whey will drip away to leave a soft cheese. Carefully gather up the corners of the muslin and squeeze any excess whey from the cheese.

Place the cheese in a shallow bowl, make an indent in the centre with the back of a spoon and fill it with olive oil. Sprinkle over the cheese fresh herbs and black pepper to taste.

Serve with slices of tomato and baby cucumber, olives and warm pitta bread. Finish with a bowl of yoghurt drizzled with runny honey.

Coffee flavoured with cardamom welcomes guests and aids the bargaining process in the souk.

The Bedouin push a cardamom pod into the spout of the coffee pot. We add either ground cardamom or slit green pods to ground coffee.

CARDAMOM COFFEE

Add ¼ teaspoon ground cardamom or 3 slit green cardamom pods per person to freshly ground coffee and make in your usual way.

Serve black with a touch of sugar for an authentic taste.

Above left **A camel rider among the ruins of Palmyra**

Right **Syrian breakfast of labneh, pitta bread, olives, slices of cucumber and tomato, yogurt with honey, and cardamom coffee.**

JEWELLED AUBERGINE

8 baby aubergines
1 medium onion, finely diced
3 garlic cloves, chopped
2 tablespoons olive oil
½ teaspoon ground cinnamon
½ teaspoon ground allspice
¼ teaspoon ground
    black pepper
2 tablespoons roughly
    chopped barberries or
    dried cherries
2 tablespoons chopped
    unsulphured dried apricots
2 tablespoons pine nuts
2 tablespoons chopped
    flaked almonds
120ml/4fl oz cooked
    basmati rice

1 tablespoon pomegranate
    molasses (see Muhammara,
    page 182) or honey
1 tablespoon butter
400g/14oz tinned chopped
    tomatoes
¼ teaspoon ground allspice
1 scant teaspoon dried mint
120ml/4fl oz vegetable stock
juice of ½ lemon
handful of chopped flat-leaf
    parsley

To serve
120ml/4fl oz natural yoghurt
    whisked with 1 crushed
    garlic clove and seasoned
    with black pepper and salt
    to taste

This recipe is a real taste of the souk: baby aubergines stuffed with pine nuts, almonds, dried apricots, barberries and rice are simmered in a spiced tomato sauce and topped with garlicky yoghurt dressing.

Sour, dried red barberries are available from Middle Eastern stores; alternatively dried cherries make a good substitute.

With a spoon scoop the flesh from the middle of the whole baby aubergines until hollow.

To make the stuffing, in a large frying pan cook the onion and garlic in the olive oil until golden. Stir in the spices, dried fruit, nuts, rice and pomegranate molasses.

Fill the aubergines with the stuffing, pressing it firmly inside until compact (any stuffing left over can be added to the tomato sauce).

Wipe the frying pan clean with kitchen paper and add the butter. When melted, lay the aubergines on their sides and fry until brown on all sides. Add the chopped tomato, allspice, dried mint and stock, and season to taste. Gently simmer, turning the aubergines and stirring occasionally (add a little water if necessary), until the aubergines are soft and the sauce has reduced.

Sprinkle the chopped parsley and lemon juice over the aubergines and serve with the seasoned yoghurt on the side.

As soon as we parked in Ma'loula, little boys ran up to the car
to offer to write our names in Aramaic for a small fee; then they
led us through a narrow rocky defile above the village to the
enchanting St Thekla Monastery. Thekla was the daughter of a
Roman governor, converted by St Paul soon after the Crucifixion.
Reputed to have been a young woman of exceptional beauty, she
had a life on the run, successfully escaping persecution and the
unwanted advances of amorous men, until arriving here to live
a life of solitude and prayer while hiding in a cave. She is one of
the most popular saints of the Christian Orient. A steep stairway
leads up to the cave that became her tomb; it is a magical place of
peace, draped in hanging ferns and the branches of trees.

A tree growing
inside the tomb of
Ma'loula

THE SYRIAN MEZE

Myriad individual colourful dishes, served to tempt the appetite before the main meal. If we are not feeling too hungry, a couple of dishes with warm flatbread make a good snack. Here are a few of our favourites.

MUHAMMARA

1 small brown pitta
   bread, ground to a fine
   breadcrumbs consistency
250g/9oz ready-roasted red
   peppers, roughly chopped
60g/2 ½ oz chopped walnuts
3 garlic cloves, finely
   chopped
½ teaspoon chilli flakes
1 teaspoon ground cumin

1 tablespoon pomegranate
   molasses or honey
1 tablespoon lemon juice
3 tablespoons olive oil, plus
   some for drizzling
finely chopped flat-leaf
   parsley and chopped
   walnuts, to garnish
warm toasted pitta bread,
   to serve

In a food processor blend the breadcrumbs with a tablespoon of water until a paste forms.

Add all the remaining ingredients and blend until finely chopped. Sprinkle with chopped parsley and walnuts and a drizzle of olive oil. Serve with warm toasted pitta bread.

Spicy roasted red pepper and walnut dip.

To keep things simple, we buy ready-roasted peppers preserved in olive oil. Pomegranate molasses is a fruit syrup used to flavour savoury and sweet dishes. It has a sweet-sour taste and can be found in Middle Eastern shops. If you have difficulty buying it, try making your own: simply simmer pomegranate juice until it reduces to the consistency of runny honey; stored in an airtight container, it will last for weeks. Alternatively replace with runny honey.

Above **View over the old city of Damascus at dusk**
Left **Syrian meze**

This dip is similar to hummus but made with fava beans, a type of broad bean (a little darker in colour and stronger in flavour), popular throughout the Middle East.

Fava beans are sold dried or precooked in tins in Middle Eastern stores, but broad beans or chickpeas also make a good alternative. We always use tinned beans.

We learned that the best way to eat *byesar* is to dip toasted pitta into za'atar spice, and then scoop up the dip.

Za'atar is used liberally throughout Syria as a condiment for dips, vegetables and rice dishes. Easy to make, it stores well in an airtight jar.

Sumac is a ground red berry, available in Middle Eastern stores. Ready-mixed za'atar is also available, if you want to opt for an easy life.

BYESAR

275g/10oz drained tinned fava beans (or broad beans, fresh or frozen)
2 garlic cloves, sliced
1 heaped teaspoon cumin seeds
¼ teaspoon cayenne pepper
5 tablespoons olive oil
a good squeeze of lemon juice

small handful of chopped mint leaves and a little extra cumin seeds, to garnish

To serve
za'atar spice mix
olive oil
toasted pitta bread

Drain the tinned beans (retaining the drained liquid) and blend in a food processor with the garlic, cumin seed, cayenne pepper, olive oil, lemon juice and 2 tablespoons of the retained water until smooth. Season to taste with salt and pepper. (If using fresh or frozen broad beans, simmer in salted water until soft, before blending with the remaining ingredients.)

Scoop into a bowl, drizzle with a little extra olive oil and garnish with chopped mint leaves and cumin seeds.

ZA'ATAR SPICE MIX

2 tablespoons sesame seeds, toasted
2 tablespoons dried thyme
2 tablespoons dried oregano
2 teaspoons sumac
½ teaspoon salt

Simply combine all the ingredients and store in a jam jar until needed.

112

PUMPKIN KIBBEH

110g/4oz fine cracked bulgur wheat
400g/14oz peeled, deseeded and cubed pumpkin
1 medium onion, chopped
2 garlic cloves, chopped
6 tablespoons plain flour
½ teaspoon ground coriander
½ teaspoon ground cinnamon
½ teaspoon ground cumin
¼ teaspoon ground white pepper
¼ teaspoon ground allspice
50g/2oz pine nuts
50g/2oz chopped walnuts
olive oil

Preheat the oven to 200°C/400°F/gas mark 6.

Place the bulgur wheat in a bowl and add enough boiling water to just cover the surface. Allow to stand for 15 minutes or so, until the water has been absorbed and the bulgur is soft.

Meanwhile boil the pumpkin in salted water until soft, drain and combine in a food processor with the onion, garlic, flour and spices.

Mix the pumpkin with the bulgur, pine nuts and chopped walnuts and season to taste.

Turn out and firmly press the mixture into a greased, shallow non-stick baking tray until approximately 1cm/½in thick.

Criss-cross the surface with a knife to make diamond-shaped bite-size pieces and then drizzle with olive oil. Bake in the preheated oven for approximately 20 minutes, until golden.

Serve dipped into tahina sauce or inside toasted pitta pockets with shredded lettuce, cucumber and tomato slices and a generous serving of tahina.

Spiced pumpkin baked with pine nuts, walnuts and bulgur wheat is delicious dipped into tahina or wrapped in unleavened bread for the ultimate sandwich on the go.

The ruins of watchtowers in the dunes around Palmyra

This super-quick recipe makes a meal in a bowl.

CHICKPEAS IN GARLICKY YOGHURT

4 garlic cloves, crushed
1 tablespoon butter
1 dessertspoon dried mint
200g/7oz natural yoghurt
1 onion, finely chopped
2 tins (400g/14oz size) of chickpeas: drain and retain one-third of the liquid

2 pitta breads, toasted and broken into bite-size pieces
3 tablespoons pine nuts, toasted
¼ teaspoon paprika
small handful of chopped dill

Fry the garlic in half the butter until golden, add the dried mint and fry for a further couple of minutes. Stir into the yoghurt and season to taste.

In the same pan, with the remaining butter, fry the onion until soft. Add the chickpeas and retained water, and simmer until the chickpeas are hot.

Line a bowl with the toasted pitta. Pour the chickpeas over the top, followed by the flavoured yoghurt. Sprinkle with the paprika, toasted pine nuts and chopped dill. Serve immediately before the pitta gets too soggy.

Tahina sauce is inseparable from Syrian cuisine. It really transforms a meal. Made with tahini (sesame seed paste), it is used as a dipping sauce or a dressing. Combine with a spoonful or two of yoghurt or mix with fried onion and cinnamon as a topping for grilled halloumi or aubergine.

TAHINA SAUCE

90ml/3fl oz light tahini
3 garlic cloves, crushed
2 tablespoons olive oil
3 tablespoons lemon juice

pinch of ground cumin and cayenne pepper
a little finely chopped flat-leaf parsley to serve

Whisk all the ingredients together. The tahini will thicken, so thin with warm water until it has a drizzling consistency. Serve with the chopped parsley sprinkled on top.

Vietnam

THE COASTAL ROUTE FROM HANOI
TO HOI AN

Pages 186–187 **Sunset over Halong Bay**

Below **A busy Hanoi street market**

Hanoi manages to blend its elegant French colonial past with a lively traditional Asian culture, some epic, almost poetic dilapidation and a dynamic new urban chic to create an evocative and irresistible cocktail. It is the quintessential Asian city.

Culinary treats can be found everywhere, from simple street stalls to trendy cafés and gourmet restaurants. To find out more about the exciting new dishes we were discovering around town, we signed up for a session in the Metropole Hotel's Vietnamese cooking school. Tam, one of the hotel chefs, took us by rickshaw on a search for ingredients deep into the city's street markets. She led us through the colourful chaos, pointing out all the products we would later use in our recipes. This was a great way to get under the skin of local life. If we had been there alone we would have felt like mere tourists, clumsily plodding past other people's lives with no chance of any interaction; instead with Tam translating and our genuine need to buy some of the produce we were real customers, tasting, prodding, squeezing and bartering with all the others. Back in the hotel's high-tech kitchen we learnt how to cook spring rolls and *pho* (noodle soup) and *che dau xanh*. When we left the kitchens to go back to being guests in the restaurant, we felt a bit like deserters joining the other side.

Travelling south to the old imperial capital of Hue on the Perfumed River, we learnt more about Vietnamese food in a private home that was a restored royal villa. The brick-floored pavilion, constructed out of dark-stained polished wood with a slate tile roof, was open on two sides to an ornate garden of lily ponds and verdant tropical foliage and connected to the rest of the house by covered walkways on stilts. Our cooking lesson was given by the young women of the family, dressed in *ao dai*, the traditional dress of Vietnamese women, made of a fitted tunic with long panels front and back over flowing silk trousers. On a hot, sultry day of non-stop torrential rain, it was all quite dream-like.

The Red Bridge Cooking School in Hoi An started with the usual market tour. Then we travelled by boat down the Bon River to an open-air classroom on the riverbank. Here we learnt a vegetarian version of Hoi An's most famous dish, *cao lau*, a bowl of rice noodles mixed with a long list of stir-fried ingredients, crunchy croutons and fresh herbs.

FOOD IN VIETNAM

The Vietnamese proverb 'Learn to eat before learning to speak' perfectly sums up the importance of cuisine in Vietnam: good, fresh food is ingrained in the very fabric and rituals of everyday life.

Between a steaming breakfast bowl of *pho* noodle soup and an evening with all the family, lunch in Vietnam is often eaten at a bustling street stall with friends and colleagues. Spring rolls are almost a national dish and sold everywhere from the yoked basket of an enterprising street seller to smart restaurants. Sweet snacks usually follow, made from mung beans and washed down with incredibly strong coffee sweetened with condensed milk.

In *bai hoi* bars, which sell a local preservative-free home-brewed beer, food is cheap and good, but watch out for dog on the menu. The Vietnamese are definitely adventurous eaters; wandering around the markets we were amazed by the insects and snakes on sale, with frogs' legs showing the influence of Vietnam's French colonial past. But traditional restaurants become vegetarian heaven on the first and fifteenth of each lunar month, as dictated by Buddhist stricture, when Buddhist meat – mock meat made from wheat gluten – is very popular on the menu.

The freshest possible ingredients are essential to the Vietnamese, who shop daily from the market for provisions. Rice is the most important ingredient. Brought to the country by the Chinese, it's grown in abundance and is always part of any meal in the form of noodles, rice wrappers or simply the unadulterated grain.

Nuoc mam, a sauce made from salted fish fermented for twelve months, is the quintessential ingredient of Vietnamese cuisine. In our recipes we substitute light soy sauce to make the recipes completely vegetarian and still create a perfect balance of sour, sweet, spicy and salty flavours.

No meal is complete without at least two or three herbs, such as basil, dill and mint, mixed with lemon grass, ginger, lime and the spices star anise, cinnamon, five-spice and cloves.

Clockwise from top left **Tofu cakes in Halong; food market in Hoi An; goods at Hanoi street market; carrying food in the old merchant quarter**

BUDDHIST MEAT STEW

450g/1lb Buddhist meat, cut into bite-size chunks
5 baby aubergines, cubed
3 tablespoons sunflower oil
1 medium red onion, sliced
3 carrots, diced
½ teaspoon ground cumin
½ teaspoon ground coriander
4 star anise
1 tablespoon brown sugar or clear honey
240ml/8fl oz vegetable stock
3 bay leaves
large handful of basil leaves, chopped

For the marinade
2 teaspoons ground turmeric
2 hot red chillies, thinly sliced

3 garlic cloves, crushed
5cm/2in piece of ginger root, peeled and cut into julienne strips
2 lemon grass sticks, crushed with a rolling pin and cut into 2cm/¾in lengths
1½ teaspoons Chinese allspice
½ teaspoon cracked black pepper
2 tablespoons light soy sauce
1 tablespoon sesame oil

To garnish and serve
110g/4oz bean sprouts
5 spring onions, sliced
handful of coriander leaves, chopped
chunks of warm baguette

Mix the marinade ingredients together and combine with the Buddhist meat and aubergine. Set to one side for 15 minutes.

Heat the sunflower oil in a wok. When hot, add the red onion and carrot. Cook until the onion is soft.

Stir in the cumin, coriander and star anise, stir-fry for a couple of minutes, and then add the marinated Buddhist meat and aubergine. Cook for a further few minutes, until browned. Then add the sugar, stock and bay leaves. Gently simmer until the aubergine is soft.

Stir in the basil leaves and season to taste.

Serve garnished with the bean sprouts, spring onion and chopped coriander, and with warm baguette to mop up the sauce.

Hoi An's history as a bustling port on the ancient spice route is reflected in this aromatic stew, spiced with turmeric and black pepper from India, bay leaves from the Levant and Chinese five-spice.

This is a traditional curry in which beef is replaced with Buddhist meat (mock meat) in keeping with Buddhist tradition, when on the first and fifteenth days of the lunar month many restaurants become vegetarian.

Mock meat is made from marinated gluten and is available in Asian stores or good health food shops (as seitan) in either tins or vacuum packs.

Boats at dawn in Halong Bay

Che shops are 'the' place to meet for a mid-afternoon sweet snack in Vietnam. *Che* is a sweet dish in which sweetened coconut milk is simmered with beans, glutinous rice or tapioca and served over ice with fruit in the summer or hot in the winter.

Vietnamese like their *che* sweet; adjust the amount of sweetening to taste.

SWEET MUNG BEAN CHE

225g/8oz hulled split golden mung beans, soaked for 3 hours and then drained and rinsed
400g/14oz tin of coconut milk
1 vanilla pod, split lengthways

¼ teaspoon salt
palm sugar (chopped), brown sugar or honey to taste
3 tablespoons toasted sesame seeds, to garnish

Cover the drained mung beans with water and simmer until soft. Drain the beans and mash or blend until puréed.

Place the coconut milk and vanilla pod in a heavy-bottomed pan and bring to simmering point. Whisk in the salt and sugar to taste and gently simmer for 5 minutes.

Stir in the puréed mung beans and simmer for a further 5 minutes. The *che* should have a thick soup-like consistency.

Serve in bowls and sprinkled with toasted sesame seeds.

One of the highlights of our journey through Vietnam was spending a couple of days on a junk drifting through the tranquil seascape of towering limestone islands in Halong Bay. It was like a living Chinese scroll painting.

BANH XEO COCONUT MILK CREPES

MAKES ABOUT 6

sunflower oil
4 shallots, sliced
2 garlic cloves, crushed
1 hot red chilli, thinly sliced
175g/6oz marinated tofu,
   sliced
175g/6oz shitake mushrooms,
   sliced
110g/4oz whole enoki
   mushrooms
2 spring onions, sliced
handful of bean sprouts

For the batter
60g/2 ½ oz rice flour
½ teaspoon ground turmeric
½ teaspoon caster sugar
240ml/8fl oz coconut milk
2 medium eggs, beaten
6 spring onions, thinly sliced

To serve
handful of coriander leaves
handful of mint leaves
nuoc cham dipping sauce

To make the batter, mix the rice flour, turmeric and caster sugar together, and gradually combine with the coconut milk and 240ml/8fl oz water until a smooth batter forms. Stir in the beaten eggs, sliced spring onions and seasoning to taste. Set to one side while you prepare the mushrooms.

Heat 3 tablespoons of sunflower oil in a non-stick frying pan. When hot, add the shallots, garlic, chilli, tofu and shitake mushrooms, and stir-fry until golden. At the last minute add the enoki mushrooms, spring onions and bean sprouts. Season to taste and tip out on to a spare plate. Wipe clean the pan with kitchen paper.

To make the pancakes, heat 1 dessertspoon of sunflower oil in the non-stick frying pan. When the oil is smoking, add a ladle of batter and swirl the pan to coat the bottom of the pan with it. Cover with a lid until the middle of the pancake is set and the outside is brown and crunchy.

Place a portion of mushroom mixture on one side of the pancake and fold in half. Cook for a further minute or so.

Repeat until all the pancake batter and filling ingredients are used up.

Serve with mint, coriander leaves and *nuoc cham* sauce.

These sizzling coconut milk crêpes, filled with mushrooms, tofu and bean sprouts, are a classic mix of French and Vietnamese cuisine.

Marinated tofu is readily available in supermarkets, health food shops and Asian stores.

Ladders in the old quarter, Hanoi

194

A dipping sauce accompanies every meal in Vietnam and a little bowl is always provided for the sauce in each place setting. *Nuoc cham* is the most popular and it also often has extra ingredients added such as grated ginger or crushed roasted peanuts.

NUOC CHAM DIPPING SAUCE

2 tablespoons brown sugar
  or honey
2 tablespoons hot water
2 tablespoons lime juice, plus
  the pulp left in the squeezer
2 tablespoons light soy sauce
1 tablespoon rice wine
  vinegar
2 teaspoons crushed garlic

2 hot red chillis,
  very finely chopped

Optional ingredients
5cm/2in piece of ginger root,
  peeled and grated
handful of skinless, unsalted
  peanuts, crushed and dry
  roasted until golden

Mix the brown sugar with the hot water until it has dissolved. Then stir in the remaining ingredients.

In the old quarter of Hanoi, we stumbled upon a street lined with *pho* noodle stalls. We joined a table at the most popular and, seated on low stools, shared the experience of slurping on a breakfast bowl of *pho* noodle soup.

Make the simple broth first and then assemble the condiments while it is simmering away. In keeping with tradition, serve the condiments in bowls on the table for people to pick and choose from.

PHO NOODLE SOUP

For the broth
1 medium onion, quartered
6 garlic cloves, sliced
5cm/2in piece of ginger root, peeled and sliced
4 star anise
2 cinnamon sticks
6 cloves
2 litres/3½ pints good vegetable stock
3 tablespoons light soy sauce
1 leek, trimmed, washed and cut into four lengths
400g/14oz medium flat rice noodles, cooked as instructed on the packet, then drained and rinsed, to serve

Condiments
150g/5oz fresh shitake mushrooms, sliced
225g/8oz diced tofu
110g/4oz bean sprouts
large handful of shredded spinach leaves
4 spring onions, thinly sliced
3 hot chillies, thinly sliced

To garnish
handful of basil leaves, roughly chopped
handful of coriander leaves
2 limes, quartered
small bowl hoisin sauce

In a saucepan dry fry the onion, garlic and ginger for a few minutes, on a low heat, stirring constantly to avoid burning. Add the spices and roast for a minute or so until aromatic.

Remove the pan from the heat, allow to cool for a few moments, and then add the stock, soy sauce, leek and seasoning to taste. Return to the heat, cover the pan and gently simmer for 20 minutes. Strain the broth and return it to the pan.

Meanwhile prepare the condiments and place in the centre of the table.

To serve, place a portion of noodles in the bottom of a deep bowl, add your choice of condiments and then ladle broth over the top (make sure it is piping hot before serving).

Garnish with basil and coriander leaves, a squeeze of lime juice and a little hoisin sauce.

Pho noodle soup

BUN CHA NOODLE SALAD

450g/1lb rice vermicelli
   noodles
300g/11oz oyster mushrooms
sunflower oil for frying
4 garlic cloves, sliced
150g/5oz mung bean sprouts
2 baby cucumbers, cut into
   julienne strips
4 spring onions, sliced
large handful of chopped
   coriander leaves
large handful of chopped
   basil leaves
large handful of chopped
   mint leaves

a large handful of finely chopped
   dill leaves
5 Cos lettuce leaves, shredded
1 teaspoon cracked black pepper
175g/6oz skinless unsalted
   peanuts, finely chopped and
   dry roasted until golden

For the dressing
60ml/2fl oz lime juice
60ml/2fl oz light soy sauce
1 tablespoon rice wine vinegar
2 teaspoons clear honey
1 garlic clove, crushed
2 hot red chillis, sliced

Soak the vermicelli noodles in boiling water until soft, drain, rinse well and set to one side.

Fry the whole oyster mushrooms in sunflower oil with the sliced garlic until golden.

Whisk the dressing ingredients together until the honey has dissolved. Combine with the noodles and the remaining ingredients.

Serve the noodles topped with the garlic-fried oyster mushrooms.

A herb and rice noodle salad topped with garlicky oyster mushrooms.

Baskets being biked to market along Highway 1, Vietnam

Mushrooms and water chestnut rice-paper spring rolls, dipped into spicy *nuoc cham* sauce (see page 195), calmed our hunger pangs on the stunning journey to Hoi An.

VIETNAMESE SPRING ROLLS

MAKES ABOUT 24
a pack of 15cm/6in round
    rice-paper wrappers
oil for shallow-frying

For the filling

50g/2oz rice vermicelli,
    soaked until soft in boiling
    water, drained, rinsed and
    cut into 2cm/¾in lengths
6 medium fresh shitake
    mushrooms, sliced
15g/¾oz dried wood ear
    mushrooms, soaked in
    boiling water until soft,
    drained and sliced

60g/2½oz tinned water
    chestnuts, drained and
    roughly chopped
1 medium carrot, grated
60g/2½oz bean sprouts
3 shallots, finely sliced
1 tablespoon soy sauce
¼ teaspoon ground black
    pepper
1 large egg, beaten

Combine all the filling ingredients together.

Now assemble the spring rolls. Dip a rice-paper wrapper in a bowl of hot water, transfer to a chopping board and then place a dessertspoon of filling slightly off-centre towards the near side. Fold the rice paper over the filling, fold in the sides and then roll to make a tightly packed spring roll. Continue in this way until the filling is finished. As you assemble the rolls, cover the completed ones with cling film until you are ready to cook them.

In a wok heat enough oil to shallow-fry the spring rolls. When hot, fry the spring rolls five at a time until golden on all sides. Drain on kitchen paper before serving with *nuoc cham* dipping sauce.

SIMPLE SOUP AND GREENS SIDE DISHES

A thin light soup and garlic-fried greens accompany most meals. Served simply with rice, they also make a satisfying lunch or supper.

THE SOUP

2 tablespoons sunflower oil

4 shallots, sliced

2 garlic cloves, crushed

2.5cm/1in piece of ginger root, peeled and cut into julienne strips

1 hot red chilli, thinly sliced

1 quantity of broth as described in the *pho* recipe on page 197, without the noodles

2 tablespoons light soy sauce

25g/1oz dried wood ear mushrooms, soaked in boiling water until soft, drained and cut into thin slices

1 small tin of straw mushrooms (225g/8oz), drained and cut in half lengthwise

6 asparagus stalks, sliced into 2cm/¾in lengths

2 medium carrots, cut into julienne strips

¼ teaspoon ground black pepper

handful of chopped coriander leaves

In a saucepan heat the oil. When hot, add the shallot, garlic, ginger and chilli, and sauté until soft.

Add the broth, soy sauce, mushrooms, asparagus and carrots. Gently simmer until the vegetables are soft. Add the chopped coriander and season to taste.

We started our days early in Hanoi, with misty morning walks around Hoan Kiem Lake, its shores a stage for the callisthenics of t'ai chi enthusiasts and its atmospheric island temple of Ngoc Son busy with devotees among clouds of incense. In Hanoi's old quarter we got lost in the maze of narrow tree-lined streets, where we ate bowls of *pho* noodle soup sitting on tiny plastic stool in pavement cafés.

Morning meditation on the shore of Hoan Kiem Lake

In Vietnam this recipe is used to stir-fry seasonal greens such as water spinach, pak choi, Chinese spinach and even pumpkin leaves. Feel free to use whatever is easily available.

THE GREENS

2 tablespoons sesame oil
6 garlic cloves, crushed
2 hot red chillies
½ teaspoon cracked
  black pepper

450g/1lb washed greens,
  roughly chopped
2 tablespoons light soy sauce

Heat the oil in a wok. When hot, add the garlic and sliced chilli, and cook until golden. Add the black pepper and greens, and stir-fry until wilted.

Stir in the soy sauce and serve immediately.

MARINATED TOFU, HERB AND LETTUCE WRAPS

500g/1lb 2oz firm tofu
Cos lettuce leaves, washed
    and cut in half widthways
2 medium carrots, cut into
    julienne strips
½ kohl rabi or white radish,
    peeled and cut into
    julienne strips
handful of mint leaves
handful of basil leaves
steamed jasmine rice, to serve

For the marinade
juice of 4 limes
3 dessertspoons clear honey or
    brown sugar
3 tablespoons soy sauce
1 tablespoon sesame oil
2 lemon grass stalks, finely
    sliced
2 hot red chillies, finely
    chopped
3 garlic cloves, finely chopped

Cut the tofu into ½cm/¼in slices, dry by pressing the slices between sheets of kitchen paper and lay in the bottom of a shallow dish.

Whisk the marinade ingredients together and pour over the tofu. Set to one side for half an hour.

While the tofu is marinating, prepare the wrap ingredients and arrange artistically on a large serving plate.

Barbecue, grill or griddle the tofu until golden brown on both sides. Pour the remaining marinade into a bowl and use as a dipping sauce for the wraps.

Serve the tofu immediately. To eat, line a lettuce leaf with mint and basil leaves, carrot and kohl rabi sticks. Place a slice of hot tofu on top and then wrap the lettuce leaf around to make a roll. Dip into the marinade sauce and enjoy with steamed jasmine rice on the side.

At lunchtime on the streets of Hue the aroma of chargrilled garlic and lemon grass fills the air. Barbecue is a popular express lunch in Vietnam.

One of the barbecued dishes is sliced marinated tofu, served hot from the grill, wrapped in crunchy lettuce leaves lined with fresh herbs and dipped into a spicy sesame and lemon grass sauce.

Marinated tofu, herb and lettuce wraps

In Hanoi we fell into the habit of taking early morning walks. Our first port of call was a café on the misty shore of the Hoan Kiem lake where, as we enjoyed a glass of Vietnamese coffee and a warm baguette, we watched the sun rise over Ngoc Son Temple.

Coffee in Vietnam is strong and smooth with a characteristic vanilla flavour, and is served slowly dripped through individual metal filters into a good serving of condensed milk. In the heat of the afternoon the filtered coffee and condensed milk are poured over ice.

Vietnamese coffee is available to buy in specialist coffee shops; or you can replicate the taste by using a strong dark roast coffee with a few drops of vanilla extract added to the condensed milk.

CAFÉ AU LAIT VIETNAMESE STYLE

fine-ground dark roast coffee
condensed milk

vanilla extract to taste
ice (optional)

We always make the coffee in the Vietnamese way, using one-cup coffee filters lined with filter paper, over a glass with a slug of condensed milk in it. Use 2 heaped dessertspoons of coffee per filter. Alternatively an espresso machine makes a good strong brew.

Whichever method you choose, pour 1cm/½in of condensed milk in the bottom of a straight glass, add a couple of drops of vanilla extract, and then carefully pour in about 4cm/1½in of the strong coffee on top.

For iced coffee simply pour the completed coffee into a separate glass half filled with ice.

Cooking school at the Metropole Hotel

Nowhere epitomises Hanoi's past and present charms more effectively than the Metropole. Rooms in the old wing are straight out of a Graham Greene novel with polished wooden floors, antique furniture and ceiling fans. Staying here felt like going back in time to the era when the hotel was the Grande Dame of Indo-China.

INDEX

Page numbers in *italic* indicate captions to illustrations.
An asterisk beside a heading indicates a dish or recipe.